Urban
Social
Structure

Urban

Social

Structure

By

James M. Beshers

The Free Press, New York
COLLIER-MACMILLAN LIMITED, LONDON

Preface

WHAT are, in fact, the implications of urbanization for human behavior? Are there, indeed, any novel implications of increasing urbanization? To sort out fact from value judgment in answering these questions is no simple task.

We shall, however, seek partial answers to the questions. In particular, we wish to know if there is an urban social structure, an over-all network of social relationships among the urban inhabitants. We seek to describe these social relationships, to see what realms of social behavior are affected by them, and to see how they are maintained and transmitted to new generations.

This essay will emphasize the following points: (1) that extension of present social theory is needed to cope with urban facts; (2) that social classes, ethnic groups and racial groups are integral parts of American urban social structure that cannot be meaningfully treated in isolation of each other; (3) that historical research, census tract research, survey research, and observational research must be integrated in an effective analysis of urban social structure; and (4) that rigorous development of theory, specifically mathematical formulation, can clarify issues presently confused.

The author contends that an integration of theoretical points of view is needed now. For all we know the problems of sociology were solved many years ago. Unless we integrate existing knowledge, and test it, we can have no notion of its deficiencies, and therefore we cannot improve it.

The author's theoretical orientation stems from the writings of Max Weber, Radcliffe-Brown, Lewin, and Asch. Special insights from Leach and Levi-Strauss have guided the development of the book. The substantive theory in Chapter Seven will remind readers more of Machiavelli, Pareto, and Veblen, than of more recent sociological theory.

ACKNOWLEDGMENTS

Numerous individuals and experiences have shaped the thinking presented in these pages—relatives, teachers, friends, colleagues, and students have contributed to the ideas in this book. Laurence Lafore, Mary Albertson, Sidney Morgenbesser, and the late Arnold Dresden were among the undergraduate teachers whose encouragement enabled me to develop and carry out my educational program. Rupert B. Vance, Daniel O. Price, Reuben Hill, and Guy B. Johnson guided my graduate sociological training along lines eventually leading to this book.

vi

The earliest forms of the book were read by my wife. Richard and Ida Simpson read and criticized the entire draft manuscript. Valuable comments also came from Walter Hirsch, Philip Marcus, Harrison White, and Louis Schneider. Without the encouragement of Stanley Reiter I would not even have attempted the mathematical appendix although he is in no way responsible for the errors therein. Carol Trumpe and Dorothy Butcher typed the manuscript. James Hawkins prepared the index.

Permission to quote from E. R. Leach, *Political Systems of Highland Burma* was granted by the Harvard University Press, the London School of Economics, and Professor Leach.

Contents

PREFACE   v

ACKNOWLEDGMENTS   vi

1. *Values, Policy, and Urban Sociology*   1

2. *Ecology and Functionalism*   13

3. *Urban Social Structure*   35

4. *Historical Processes*   61

5. *Social Structure and Residential Areas*   87

6. *Consequences of Spatial Distribution*   109

7. *A Theoretical Model for Urban Social Structure*   127

8. *Urban Social Organization*   159

APPENDIX—*Mathematical Aspects*   179

INDEX   205

Urban
Social
Structure

1

Values, Policy, and
Urban Sociology

A city brings forth a myriad of responses in human beings—
it is the locus of excitement, entertainment, or refinement to
some; of filth, disease, and evil to others. Some idolize the city,
some wish to reform the city, and some would like to turn the
clock back to an era in which cities were a less prominent aspect
of human life.

These various value judgments underlie most discussions of
urban life. Popular thought, public policy, and somber academic

1

treatises are all phrased in language suggestive of these underlying values. We must perform a self-conscious analysis of such value judgments and select our terminology with care before we atttempt our own discussion of the city. Only then can we guard ourselves from tangling fact with value judgment.

Value judgments often enter science as guides to public policy. Not infrequently, we find that people advocate those policies by which they stand to gain, and the arguments advanced in favor of these policies tend to reflect the interests of a particular segment of the population. Such arguments merit close examination. Our first problem, then, is to understand the relationship among values, public policy, and sociology as they impinge upon urban social life.

In twentieth-century America, municipal reform movements have proliferated and gained strength until now, at mid-century, they represent a significant, perhaps dominant, public attitude toward urban life. Good government, city managing, city planning, and urban renewal all seem to be aspects of a common reform impulse. Today, most research on the city is guided by this impulse—administrators, planners, and social workers constitute the audience for this research.

From the slum on one hand to the suburb on the other, the characteristics of residential areas and their effect upon the overall city must attract the attention of urban reformers, and social characteristics of these residential areas are of particular interest. The research literature reviewed in this essay is of some relevance to the practical concerns of urban reform.

In general, sociologists have maintained an interest in the patterns of social life emerging in the city and in the consequences that might entail for future generations from the perpetuation of these patterns. However, rather abstract and theoretical endeavors characterize the writings in this vein; empirical research on the city is seldom integrated into the discussion. Indeed, the city itself is of only incidental significance in many of the most recent sociological works.

2

In contrast to these writings, this study will have a restricted scope of theoretical investigation. Systematic examination of empirical findings will constitute the main body of the volume. Yet this restriction does not simplify the theoretical task as much as might be suspected. The close examination of a smaller problem will reveal intricacies that have escaped more general investigation. The next two chapters will develop this approach more fully.

Further, this study deals explicitly with urban phenomena. The existence of a void in urban sociological theory has been widely lamented of late (Sjoberg, 1959). This volume may help to correct the situation.

In working one's way through both practical and theoretical writings on urban life, one is struck by the degree to which the various viewpoints represent personal preferences for either urban or rural life. Blanket approval of one way of life coupled with blanket disapproval of the other is commonly found. It is well to examine the bases for such prejudices before proceeding to a more intensive analysis of the literature.

At least three kinds of expression of hostilities to the city can be uncovered. First, a distaste for the "mob" and the "masses" has long been firmly entrenched in European thought. The precedent for such distaste can be found in Greek thought, especially in Plato. This distaste is most pronounced among members and admirers of the aristocracy in western Europe although it is shared by the middle classes as well. A single event, the French Revolution, dominates the later writing in this vein. The Paris mob, though tamed by Napoleon's whiff of grapeshot, has served as a combined symbol of political fear and aesthetic revulsion in the minds of many people. The city, as the locus of mob action, has been widely viewed with suspicion.

A second expression of hostility toward the city is found among the boosters of rural life. This "return to nature" theme can also be found in European thought. The glorification of agriculture as a way of life is found on both sides of the Atlantic.

3

A theory of the past as a "Garden of Eden" seems to be an essential ingredient of this view—once upon a time man lived in a paradisaical garden, but he since has been driven out. All things idyllic are associated with the garden, and subsequent events are necessarily viewed with suspicion. Henry Nash Smith has examined these themes in American literature (Smith, 1957). The following quotation from a self-styled Jeffersonian, James B. Lanman, expresses the flavor of this literature:

> If, as has been remarked by a distinguished statesman, cities are the sores of the political body, where the bad matter of the state is concentrated, what healthful habitudes of mind and body are afforded by agricultural enterprise! The exhilarating atmosphere of a rural life, the invigorating exercise afforded by its various occupations, the pure water, the abundance of all the necessaries of subsistence, leading to early and virtuous marriages, all point to this pursuit as best adapted to the comfort of the individual man. Its beneficial bearing upon the state is no less obvious. The agriculturalist, removed from the pernicious influences that are forever accumulated in large cities, the exciting scenes, which always arise from large accumulations of men, passes a quiet and undisturbed life, possessing ample means and motives thoroughly to reflect upon his rights and duties, and holding a sufficient stake in the soil to induce him to perform those duties both for himself and his country (Smith, 1957, p. 162).

Sentiments such as these appear to underlie most favorable discussions of the folk element in American society, especially where a contrast between folkways and urban life is being considered. In part, these sentiments reflect the lives of several generations of Americans. Born and reared in a rural setting, they carry fond memories of their rural youth with them throughout their subsequent careers. The present, fraught with the uncertainty revealed to their adult eyes, necessarily seems evil in contrast with the past.

A third expression of hostility toward the city, often combined with the above, extolls the virtues of the small town. The

4

exalted position of the small town in nineteenth-century America seems to have few counterparts elsewhere. Several Protestant denominations became so closely identified with the small town that its life came to resemble Calvin's Geneva. Of course, the Puritan tradition of New England was a direct source of this influence on the town. Moral condemnation of the city, expressed in the stern language of sin with vivid references to Sodom and Gomorrah, is the form taken by this third kind of hostility. The successes of the Anti-Saloon League mark the high tide of this influence in American life (Odegard, 1928). However, the middle class distaste for the immoral urban lower classes continues to have significant implications. These sentiments of disapproval are associated with the sociological notion of social disorganization. They also seem implicit in the antiseptic rebuilding of the city that the Editors of *Fortune* comment on in *The Exploding Metropolis* (1958).

Two main expressions of values favorable to the city can be identified. The first has its source in a preference for participating in and observing of certain activities that flourish in the city —art, music, drama, and so forth. These distinctive and unique contributions of civilization can be achieved only in an urban context. To share in these contributions, to be sophisticated, one must reside in the city. The alternative is "the idiocy of rural life," as expressed by Marx.

The second expression of favorable values is most pronounced in ideas of political liberalism. The city as locus of individual freedom is emphasized in this view. Individual opportunity is unfettered by ties of kinship so that individual merit may be properly rewarded. Durkheim expressed this view in his contrast between the mechanical solidarity of traditional societies and the organic solidarity of contemporary urban industrial societies (Durkheim, 1947). In the former, the individual must conform to the strictures of society, while in the latter, certain rights of the individual are preserved against

5

society. Heterogeneity and deviant persons are not necessarily condemned by political liberals. On the contrary, such manifestations of social change will usually be viewed by them as progress.

Perhaps the complications resulting from these value positions can be illustrated by a discussion of the term "natural" as it is used to justify the superiority of rural life. In one sense, natural seems to imply traditional or customary, that which is natural is that which was done in the past. In this sense, then, any change is unnatural and therefore a change for the worse. But the past for one person is not the same as the past for another. A recent migrant to the city may find the noise of streetcars and subways unnatural, his sleep will be disturbed, but the vacationing urbanite may find the chirping of a single cricket sufficient to disturb his sleep.

Although all of these positions can be found in sociological literature, two positions hostile to urban life have been particularly significant in recent urban sociology. As mentioned previously, the preference for rural life has been expressed in the notion of a folk culture, while hostility toward urban lower classes has been expressed in the notion of social disorganization. These two positions deserve more detailed consideration since both are firmly imbedded in sociology.

The systematic contrast between rural and urban social life has its roots in some of the earliest sociological formulations. Nineteenth-century sociologists contrasted the social characteristics of the society emerging around them with the characteristics of previous historical periods. The contrast was often expressed in a typology—a dichotomy abstracting the most distinctive property of each era. The earliest of these schemes were simple evolutionary devices, often social prophecies, and therefore were of dubious value for descriptive purposes. Comte's contrast between Theological and Positive stages in evolution and Spencer's distinction between military and industrial society both reflect these tendencies.

Subsequent typologies became more analytic in intent. Tönnies, for example, expressed different types of social relationship in his distinction between *Gemeinschaft* and *Gesellschaft*— roughly equivalent to a distinction between personal and impersonal. These notions survive in the categories of descriptive sociology today.

Odum and Redfield extended these typologies with the description of a folk society. Programs of empirical research were initiated, but the characteristics of the folk society were the primary interest of this research. Therefore, these programs were less enlightening as to the characteristics of urban social life. Nevertheless, the sociological conception of urban life has been greatly influenced by the views of Odum and Redfield.

Probably these typologies have limited usefulness as guides for contemporary urban social research. Current research efforts are aimed at description of many different cities. Census data are being supplemented by direct observation techniques. The scope of the variation of social characteristics among cities of different sizes, economic structures, and cultural contexts must be determined empirically before any universal or distinctive elements of urban life can be distinguished.

In sum, whatever the merits of the folk society as a place to live in, contrast of folk with urban ways of life does not help us in the detailed study of the city itself.

The single concept, social disorganization, has served as a theoretical framework for numerous sociological inquiries. Among American sociologists, social disorganization is used to describe the city in general, urban lower classes more specifically, and the Burgess zone in transition most specifically. Social disorganization is assumed to exist in an urban area, and then bits and parts of urban life are listed as consequences of it—crime rates, suicide rates, alcoholic-consumption rates, mental-disease rates, and so on. But these rates are themselves the defining characteristics of social disorganization, thus a circularity is introduced: Disorganization is inferred from its consequences, but then these consequences are imputed to disorganization. Direct definitions of disorganization, independent of its consequences, are not widely used. Only a Durkheim, with meticulous methodology, careful theoretical formulation, and exhaustive examination of data could infer characteristics of social organization from such rates alone. However, Durkheim did not explain all variations in suicide rates in terms of anomie, much less identify the phenomenon of suicide with anomie.

As an alternative to the disorganization approach, we may assume that social organization exists. Then the characteristic variations in organization and their consequences can be directly determined by empirical procedures. Lack of organization can be considered as an empirically discoverable possibility. Thus the assumption of social organization subsumes the disorganization approach while avoiding its weaknesses.

The value problem becomes even more pressing if we turn to an examination of urban reform programs. Any reform program can be analysed into two kinds of propositions. One kind states the values (or ends) underlying the program objectives, the other kind describes the action program (or means) by which the program objectives will be achieved. To these two kinds of propositions must come two separate justifications. First, the values must be shown to be desirable (to whom and how depends upon the political system and culture in a given society). Secondly, the action programs must be designed so that they express these value, objectives rather than different or perhaps entirely unexpected values.

The first kind of proposition leads to several difficulties. In a democratic society, heterogeneous values often must be welded together into a single program. Caution must be exerted to avoid the inclusion of values that are punitive toward particular segments of society, and in this connection knowledge of the sources of values is very helpful.

The second kind of proposition, which describes the action programs, under analysis turns out to be an implicitly theoretical proposition of social science. All of these kinds of propositions may be cast in the following form: if x is changed then y will change, where x is the action program and y is a form of human behavior. The resulting y is the desired state of affairs so that, in general, if y represents an evil, it will decline, whereas if y is desirable, it will increase (changes in the educational system, in the city planning program, or in leading community organizations may serve as examples of changes in x; while a decline in delinquency may suffice to illustrate a change in y.) Social scientists should best be able to evaluate these propositions since they are statements of social theory and therefore (hopefully) amenable to verification by social research. Thus, the connection between abstract social theory and applied social reform may be much closer than it usually appears. Unfortunately, most reform-oriented research consists mainly of shocking description intended to obtain support for a particular action program. The evaluation of action programs is a relatively recent endeavor.

Urban reform programs present a troublesome problem when the definition of x and of y is attempted. Should x or y contain references to the city or to urban phenomena? Or should they merely refer to the program or behavior directly without including the locale in which it takes place? If x is the educational system of a city, is the city itself of crucial significance? Do the educational systems of cities have special features contrasting with other educational systems? What aspects of a particular locality affect human behavior?

Different reform programs might be envisioned that depend upon the importance attached to the social structure of the city in these propositions. If the city is merely made up of individuals and is a passive locus for their activities, then considerations of the psychology of the individual are sufficient to evaluate these propositions. But if particular forms of behavior are specific to

9

the city, more than these psychological considerations must enter in; further social and cultural characteristics of cities would have to be considered.

But can the city itself be thought of either as a cause or an effect, an x or a y? Or is the city a mediating or contributing influence entering indirectly into the causal relationship between x and y? Or is x or y a property of cities alone? There are different schools of thought in sociology on this point. The human ecologists would assign greater importance to the city than would most other sociologists. Students of social stratification would assign some importance to the city, at least as an indirect influence, but social psychologists would consider it of minimal importance. The merits of these positions will be evaluated in subsequent chapters. It is sufficient for the present to note that very different practical consequences may follow from these different positions.

An example of a past school of thought in urban reform may help to clarify the above discussion. Among city planners, especially those with a primarily architectural background, the physical features of the city could be viewed as ultimate causal factors. Thus, the city planners might say that if the slums were replaced with bright new buildings juvenile delinquency would decline. The action program x would consist of tearing down old buildings and constructing new buildings.

The Editors of *Fortune*, in *The Exploding Metropolis*, call attention to the shortcomings of this architectural determinism. One of their respondents speaks as follows:

> Once upon a time we thought that if we could only get our problem families out of those dreadful slums, then papa would stop taking dope, mama would stop chasing around, and Junior would stop carrying a knife. Well, we've got them in a nice new apartment with modern kitchens and a recreation center. And they're the same bunch of bastards they always were (Editors of Fortune, 1958, p. 106).

We will not attempt a general solution of the reform problem in this essay. Instead, a narrower focus upon social structure will be maintained. Two general problems will be pursued. First, the social characteristics of residential areas will be examined to determine what light they can throw on the general social structure of the city. Secondly, the influence of area or location upon social structure and behavior will be assessed. This second problem will lead us to partial insights into the larger problem of the influence of the city itself.

In sociology these problems for the most part have been left to human ecologists. But the literature on stratification, caste, and class is also clearly relevant. Unfortunately, these two literatures are couched in entirely different theoretical terminologies, and currently exist independently. The next chapter will be devoted to an exposition, comparison, and unification of these two separate theoretical traditions.

In sum, then, our problem has been placed within a general context of concern. The characteristic value judgments underlying discussions of cities have been indicated. The implications of values for a reform program have also been discussed. But reform equally consists of an action program, and an evaluation of this action program falls within the sphere of social science. The significance of the city itself for the success of the action program is not entirely clear. The focus of this study will be narrowed to the relationship between residential areas and social structure. The general implications of this relationship lie behind us, ahead lies the statement of it in sociological theory.

2

Ecology and Functionalism

IN this chapter we shall seek to establish a relationship between ecology and functionalism. In order to probe the relationship between social structure and residential areas, we will review research guided by both schools of thought. However, we cannot easily relate these findings, since they are couched in entirely different terminology.

We shall see that both ecology and functionalism are attempts to explain regularities in the behavior of large groups of people. The characteristic activities of these people, the characteristic relationships among these people, and the consequences of these characteristics constitute a common problem area of concern. Following a practice in economics, we shall call this common macroscopic problem *the aggregate problem*.

The aggregate problem arises whenever attention is shifted from the study of individual or separate units to the study of combination or agglomeration of these units. Repeated experience has shown that conclusions based on the study of separate units may be of little value for the study of the combination of units into an aggregate. For sociologists, the relevant units may be persons, groups, communities, or societies. Durkheim's polemic insistence upon social facts is an assertion that the aggregate behavior of humans cannot be explained by the study of isolated individual humans (Durkheim, 1950).

The aggregate that particularly interests us is the city. Let us, for the moment, define a city as a large community. In turn, a community has been defined as "the structure of relationships through which a localized population provides its daily requirements (Hawley, 1950), and as "that collectivity the members of which share a common territorial area as their base of operations for daily activities" (Parsons, 1951). How, then, does the city, as an aggregate, affect the activities of persons and groups within it?

These definitions both contain the clue to the difficulties ahead. The community is at once a social entity and a territorial entity. But the relationship between social structure and area has not been explicitly developed in sociological theory. Indeed, as noted in the previous chapter, these two topics have gone their separate ways. Areas are the province of human ecology, a specialty relying upon the concepts of animal ecology for much of its theoretical content. Social-structure analysis has developed in two directions. One direction, at the societal level of analysis, employs the biological analogy of "system" within which various structures and their functions are identified. The other direction, at the group level of analysis, is concerned primarily with the

14

social-psychological consequences of social structure. Both directions are called functionalism. Merton's work illustrates both aspects of this type of analysis of social structure.

A link between areas and social structure is reported to be discoverable empirically by many investigators. The social characteristics of residential areas are correlated with social class (Mack, 1951). Thus Warner, *et al*, for example, use the characteristics of a residential area as an index of social class (Warner, Meeker, and Eells, 1949). However, an established correlation does not constitute a theory. In Chapters Three and Four the social-class materials will be examined more intensively. For the present, we need only note that this kind of finding is not a substitute for theoretical development.

We first must state the connection between ecology and functionalism. In particular, we need to see how the theory of each treats the aggregate problem in sociology. Research on both residential areas and social structure can be utilized and coordinated within such a framework.

Four tasks must be undertaken before the connection between functionalism and ecology can be established directly: first, we must review some fundamental assumptions of sociological research; second, we must then define our major concepts; third, we must examine the conceptual system of human ecology; and fourth, we must also study the conceptual system of functionalism. This may seem an indirect approach, but the fundamentals must be agreed upon before the more intricate aspects of the problem can be made clear.

The minimal assumptions of sociology must be methodological rather than factual. We can state how we go about our work, but we must do so in a manner that does not prejudge the results of the work; for if the results were already known, then we need not have undertaken the work at all. Any assumptions that we make will have some consequences for our subsequent empirical work, these assumptions will become part of the model we employ. We must select first those assumptions that least prejudice our inquiry, and then admit further assumptions only if supported by empirical criteria. Each concept in sociology is an implicit assumption, namely, that some part of the empirical world can be identified with it.

We begin by observing a series of events in time. Next, we observe relationships among the events. These relationships must be empirically demonstrable, and the empirical demonstration of relationships is measurement. Next, we name and classify the events, that is, we delineate units among the events accordings to boundaries that are themselves relationships. Examples of this kind of relationship include similar-dissimilar, more similar-less similar, and degree of similarity. The degree of similarity permits us to define variables. The relationship of similarity to dissimilarity is important with respect to position in time.

We also observe relationships among relationships. Over a period of time we observe the repetition of similar relationships —regularities. At one time we observe an over-all pattern of relationships. We may define a structure, in general, as a pattern of relationships persisting over time.

The original events are explained if the time relationships among regularities can be specified, the regularities among regularities, so to speak. The simplest explanation of this is given in the traditional form of the causal law, if x then y; often more complex mathematical statements are involved.

We shall use cause in a general sense. Therefore, when we say that we seek the "causes" of certain events, we merely mean that we would like to explain the events in the above sense (if x then y). In our subsequent discussion, the term "cause" will be used to remind us that our concern is with relationships in time, not timeless correlations (Lenz, 1958).

So far these assumptions may seem simple enough. If they were sufficient to define the methodology of the social sciences, we

16

might wonder that any research remained to be done. Unfortunately, any number of complications could be introduced at this point. Three seem to be particularly appropriate.

First, the number of possible ways to define units is so large that it might well be regarded as infinite; the same can be said for relationships. Particular investigators will make their own choices (Lewin, 1935).

Second, the sheer quantity of events, no matter how one defines units, is enormous. Some restriction of the field of inquiry must be made at the outset. The real world may be a single, continuous process, but we will have to work with part of it. Such restrictions may introduce distortions in the section observed, or, more accurately, they may leave out the relationships that in fact are important to the explanation. Here again, the investigator must make his choice, and the choice of units and relationships partially determines the restrictions.

Third, the investigator must always work with partial information. Error is always present. All measurements cannot be made simultaneously and repeatedly. The obscuring effect of weather conditions upon astronomical observation is similar to the effect of physical obstructions, such as architecture, upon social observation. This third point also follows from both the first two. The selection of units and relationships and the restriction of inquiry both result in partial information.

These complications, especially the third, help us to see the special role theory must play. If we had complete information, theory would be merely a particular form of description, a special organization of data. Given partial information, one must bridge the gaps with theoretical formulations. Some of the theoretical formulations will not be demonstrated readily by empirical materials, yet they are necessary to fill the gaps; if the formulations do not yield testable hypotheses, however, they cannot fill the gaps. Theory connects that which we can observe or measure.

The need for restriction of the field of inquiry helps us to understand the usage of the word "system." In its simplest form the system is simply the set of units, relationships, and data to which attention is restricted. In order to avoid distortion, however, the restriction should not be arbitrary. One should be able to identify and define empirical boundaries for the system as for any other unit.

The effort to define distinct systems of variables and then to study the relationships within and among these variables has led in economics to the distinction between exogenous and endogenous variables (Simon, 1957). Endogenous variables are contained within the system upon which analysis is focused; there are reciprocal relationships among these endogenous variables. Exogenous variables are not in the system under analysis. The implications of these for the endogenous variables is under investigation, but not the inverse relationships. To illustrate in simple causal terminology, if we wish to examine both propositions "if x then y" and "if y then y," then only y is contained in the system.

When the word system is used in this study it will usually have the rather general meaning suggested above. But a fascination with biological analogies has led to a more restrictive meaning of system in sociology (Merton, 1949). Equilibrium can simply refer to a set of stable relationships among variables. As such, it is on the same empirical footing as any other statement of relationships. But the system model currently in vogue assumes equilibrium as essential to the definition of the system. If equilibrium is destroyed, the system is destroyed. Biological organisms die unless a complex arrangement of causal relationships is maintained. Therefore, a system goal, such as life maintenance (homeostasis), can be regarded as defining the equilibrium conditions. The function of the parts of the system is to contribute to equilibrium maintenance. But the assumption of a system goal may often be gratuitous in sociology.

With this methodological framework in hand, we can proceed to definitions. "Social structure" and "social organization" are the main terms to be considered; they will be most helpful in clarifying the aggregate problem.

Structure has already been defined as a persisting pattern of relationships among units. To define social structure it is only necessary to specify the appropriate relationships and units. Let us state that social structure is made up of social relationships. If we take persons as units, we can state that a social relationship exists between two persons if: (1) the two persons are aware of each other; and (2) the behavior of the persons toward each other exhibits regularities. This definition can be extended if we consider classes of persons made up in such a way that similar regularities are observed whenever a person from one class establishes a social relationship with a person from the other class. Such classes of persons define social positions. The reciprocal relationships between clerk and customer and husband and wife are examples. The holders of these positions need not be aware of all holders of reciprocal positions —all clerks need not be aware of all customers.

Social structure is thus the over-all pattern or network of social relationships that recur among a designated set of persons. Some authors would like to extend the definition further to include relationships among organized groups of persons. This extension seems unnecessary. The definition given permits the class of persons to be specialized in a number of ways. Certainly, organized groups are one expression of specialization. But the relationships among the persons in the groups are the point of interest, not the relationship among the groups themselves.

Much terminological confusion in sociology has resulted from the ambiguities of meaning of "social organization," especially as social organization tends to overlap or encompass the meaning of social structure. At least three main referents for social organization can be identified. First, value or normative integration is implied by the social-disorganization school (Cohen, 1959). Second, the organization of activities toward goals, the intermeshing of these activities, is the focus of attention in studies of industrial organization. Third, the over-all pattern of social relationships, in a sense close to that used in discussion or definitions of social structure, is implied by many text book writers.

All of these referents will appear in this study, but it is convenient to restrict the definition of social organization to the second one. This choice is suggested by Radcliffe-Brown (Radcliffe-Brown, 1952, p. 11). Thus the units of social organization are activities, the relationships of concern among them are their intermeshing to achieve goals. Equilibrium need not be assumed as necessary to social organization, though it may be assumed for particular problems. Efficiency, the way the intermeshing of the activities can affect achievement of goals, is often more interesting in organizational research. All the participants can speak different languages and hate each other and still get out their work. Social relationships can exist among persons performing these activities but they are not necessary. The fact that workers on one shift may never even see workers on another shift does not suggest a lack of organization.

This definition of social organization is designed to contain the important features of the division of labor. Parsons expresses roughly the same idea with his notion of ecological system (Parsons, 1951, pp. 93–94). Hawley's use of symbiotic relationships could be applied to the relationships among the persons engaged in intermeshed activities (Hawley, 1959, Chaps. III, XII).

Social organization may refer most simply to a single concrete unit such as a factory; it is convenient, however, in this essay to extend the definition, thus social organization will be used to refer to the relationships among such units or groups as well. The competition among various groups will be included in social organization. The lack of clearly defined goals is a quite troublesome aspect of this generalization, but the gain of being able to treat such large amorphous aggregates as cities will outweigh the disadvantages.

Social organization, as defined above, depends in the first instance upon causal relations. The intermeshing of activities in time to achieve a goal depends upon the causal relationships between one activity and the next. Social relationships can affect these causal relationships and therefore enter the causal chain. But the participants need not be aware of the causal relationships that relate their activities. Within a particular organization, persons designated as leaders will attempt to comprehend and control all of the causal relationships that affect efficiency. Whether the leaders ever really understand these relationships is something else, but certainly the rank and file are not necessarily much concerned.

Social structure and social organization have distinct empirical referents. In practice, we will find that social structure can be studied without paying much attention to social organization. But the converse is not true. Studies of social organization will have to pay close attention to social structure.

A few more terms will be used with the meanings ordinarily attached to them. In particular, reference will be made to the cultural system, the environmental system, and the behavioral or action system. The "cultural system" is composed of the knowledge, values, and beliefs held by designated persons, as well as the objects symbolizing the foregoing. The cultural system need not be uniform, integrated, shared by all persons, nor transmitted by an inflexible social heredity.

The "environmental system" contains everything nonsocial. Propositions dealing exclusively with physics, chemistry, and biology (not human) refer to the environmental system. If we examine the social or symbolic implications of an object, we are not dealing solely with the environmental system. The distinction is a differentiation between the causal assertions of natural science and those of social science. Obviously, physical events can affect social events, but it is convenient for our purposes to separate them.

The "behavioral" or "action system" is the subject matter of social psychology. Propositions dealing with the behavior of individuals in groups are considered within this system. In particular, problems of purposive behavior, learning, personality formation, and perception may be dealt with in the context of the group of persons immediately in contact with an individual.

The behavioral system does not deal directly with the facts of social aggregates. Some aspects of aggregate behavior can be explained in behavioral terms. But our other concepts are directly derived from considering humans in the aggregate. A psychologist, Asch, may be quoted in order to clarify this point:

> The study of social behavior is part of the task of a general psychology. Its facts and principles cannot be derived from the study of behavior outside the social setting. At the same time a theory of society cannot be exclusively psychological. The interrelations among the actions of the members of society reveal regularities and tendencies that can be studied in their own right; these are the province of the social disciplines. They furnish a knowledge of the social environment that psychology needs for the same reason that it relies upon physics and biology for a knowledge of the physical conditions that surround us. In turn the social disciplines need a better understanding of the psychological facts, of the ways in which humans understand the conditions and forces among which they act (Asch, 1952, p. 38).

We now have the equipment for the task laid out at the beginning of the chapter: the relation of ecology and functionalism as theoretical systems. In particular, the use of both to deal with the problem of the aggregate. We wish to understand the ways in which humans comprehend the forces about them; yet we also wish to understand regularities of behavior in the aggregate of which humans may yet be unaware.

Human ecology, with few roots in social science, is an effort to employ biological concepts in the explanation of human behavior. Let us consider some of the main features of this school of thought.

First, and probably least successful, is the effort to distinguish between the symbiotic relationship and the social relationship. Park distinguished a moral or cultural order from a competitive or symbiotic order (Park, 1952, essays 12, 14, and 19). The moral order was based on communication and was supported by the sentimental aspects of social relationships and by the stability and integration of the culture. The symbiotic order was based upon competition for resources: a symbiotic relationship being essentially a competitive relationship within the sphere of economic activity.

The distinction Park is attempting is probably best expressed in two different ways. Most sociologists today use the concept "social relationship" to include both personal and impersonal relationships. The personal relationships are ends in themselves, whereas the impersonal relationships are means, for instance, instrumental or transactional. The concepts of expectation, role, and norm may be used to analyse either kind of social relationship. A competitive relationship may simply be an impersonal relationship.

On the other hand, not all the meaning of symbiosis is contained in impersonal relationships. Perhaps the idea of interdependence in a network of causal relationships more adequately expresses the biological analogy. In particular, interdependence within the economic sphere seems to be the crucial point. Certainly most studies using the symbiotic relationship to describe social events have dealt with the economic relations among groups of people who have little social contact rather than with relations among individual persons.

The second feature, very alive today under another name

23

(functional prerequisites), is the environment-organism relationship. The biological concept of food-chain emphasizes the fact that the environment for one organism consists in part of other organisms. The environmental system is related to the social system through this concept of resources. The economic system includes the organization of human activities in the goal of resource utilization—extraction, refinement, and distribution of resources. An economic system implies a number of persons engaged in various activities that must be intermeshed adequately to achieve system goals. This intermeshing, however, is achieved through complex social processes; culture, social structure, and other concepts must enter into the explanation of how these processes work. Park failed to conceptualize adequately the resource-utilization process as a social process, ignoring in particular the economic system. Indeed, ineffective relationships between ecological concepts and social concepts have characterized most ecological writing. To state that ecological processes are subsocial is to evade the issue.

The urban ecologists have emphasized one aspect of physical resources in their research—space. The description of land use as revealed in processes of invasion, succession, and segregation became their central research theme. The understanding and statement of relationships to the economic system were achieved through the study of land values and transportation: The map became the essential research tool.

Specifically social explanations were omitted in this form of research. Theoretical explanations for the social processes being studied fell back on stating that land values were the result of competition for scarce resources. An economic explanation of these phenomena was taken as sufficient. Few people asked why particular locations were desirable, or at least, why particular people might desire them. Park treats the problem in only one essay (Park, 1952, pp. 170, 177).

Two explanations of land use in social terms have been put

24

forward. Form suggests that the urban power structure can control the movement of the processes of land use (Form, 1954). He believes that a study of city government, city planners, and real-estate organizations would be very helpful in explaining its patterns and processes. Certainly, zoning is hard to conceptualize in strictly economic terms. Firey argues that culture or sentiment can serve as a brake to the economic processes (Firey, 1946). Beacon Hill and the Boston Common should have been put to different uses if land economics alone were considered, but sentiment prevented the change.

Another social explanation would apply specifically to the changing population of residential areas. The processes of invasion, succession, and segregation are in part reflections of social distance among ethnic groups and classes. This point will receive more attention in the next two chapters.

At this point a third main feature of human ecology must be considered. The reciprocal nature of the causal relationship between resources and human behavior is not clearly recognized by present-day human ecologists. Malthus, who stated this relationship in its classic form, may well be regarded as the original ecologist. On the one hand we may study the factors influencing the supply of resources, including the social factors. On the other hand we may take the supply of resources itself as a causal factor and investigate its consequences for social events. In particular, we might find that a decrease in the supply of resources would affect human behavior in such a way that a further decrease in resources would take place. The arguments of Malthus on the relationship between resources and population take this reciprocal form.

Further, we should note the nature of Malthus' use of resources in his argument—if there is no food, then there are no people. A negative assertion must be made. In general, when a geographer or ecologist says that the environment is a limiting factor upon human behavior, he means that this kind of negative assertion can be defended, but that the positive assertion (if there is food, then there are people) cannot be defended. Ecologists should make more systematic use of such negative assertions.

Perhaps the fourth, and most significant, development in the field of human ecology is the recently emerging identification of it with Durkheim's social morphology. This development explicitly considers social organization and social structure as aggregate social concepts and also considers the reciprocal causal relationships between biophysical environment and social organization. In this form, human ecology becomes one of several possible approaches to the study of aggregate social relationships rather than a set of nonsocial explanations for social processes. Duncan and Schnore are the most active advocates of this point of view (Duncan, 1959; Schnore, 1958).

In summary, human ecology has suffered in the past from two weaknesses: Inadequate conceptualization of causal relationships has been coupled with inadequate conceptualization of social processes.

Before we attempt to offer an alternative conceptualization, let us turn to functionalism. Further difficulties in conceptualization of aggregate social relationships will be revealed shortly.

Since Merton's exposition of functionalism has been the most influential statement of it in American sociology, we shall examine it in some detail (Merton, 1949). The essential feature of functionalism is its reliance upon an organismic analogy. A system with the goal of system maintenance is assumed to exist. The structure of the system consists of the names and locations of the various parts of the system, which are more or less stable over time. The function of the structure is to maintain the system goal, that is, to maintain a state of equilibrium. Each unit of structure is examined in turn to see how it contributes to the over-all system goal. One imagines each unit, in turn, re-

26

moved from the system, and what the consequences of its removal might be. Either another structural unit will be found to assume the missing function, or the system will die. This analysis is both static and inflexible in its view of social systems.

Two main criticisms will be developed. First, functionalism is only a special aspect of causal analysis. If this point is lost sight of, the heuristic merits of the system model are abandoned in favor of a scientific orthodoxy. Second, the social-psychological assumptions of funtionalism, especially those expressed in the distinction between manifest and latent functions, are totally inadequate.

The first point was anticipated earlier in this chapter in the discussion of methodological assumptions. In that discussion, the system model was introduced as a set of rather restrictive assumptions that might be made after sufficient assumptions for explanation, or causal analysis, had already been introduced. In that context, functionalism is only a particular way of going about causal analysis, for functionalism requires all the assumptions that any causal analysis must, and more besides.

The same point can be made in Merton's terms. While he explicitly differentiates function from cause, he ultimately defines function as consequence for system. While function-consequence differs from a simplified view of cause-effect in that reciprocal relationships may be admitted, it is hard to see how a sophisticated view of causation is to be differentiated from function. If x has consequences for y, then x and y are parts of some larger, on-going causal system. That Merton's use of consequence is not very different from cause is suggested by his theorem:

> . . . any attempt to eliminate an existing social structure without providing adequate alternative structures for fulfilling the functions previously fulfilled by the abolished organization is doomed to failure (Merton, 1949).

27

Finally, a similar point of view with regard to Merton's functionalism is developed by Nagel:

> But to say that the function of some organ in a living body (or of some part in a machine) is such-and-such, is to assert that the organ and some of its activities (and correspondingly for a machine part) is instrumental to maintaining some state or process of the organism, so that the occurrence of this state or process is causally dependent upon that organ and its behavior (Nagel, 1956, p. 249).

While recognizing several usages of the term "function" in biology, Nagel proceeds to argue that all of these usages can be translated into the more familiar language of necessary and sufficient conditions.

When we turn to the intricacies of manifest and latent functions, we find a further reason for preferring cause to function in a statement of methodology. Manifest functions are seen and/or intended. Latent functions are unseen and unintended. But manifest functions are evidently the consequences of people's actions, otherwise they could not be intended. Why not say they are the effects of action? This is the language in which the individual expresses himself. Humans are continually reducing the world around them to cause and effect relationships. To the extent that we wish to study the intentions of behavior we might as well employ the language in which they are expressed.

Suppose we consider manifest and latent causal relationships. We can simplify matters further by restricting ourselves to the case of recognized and unrecognized causal relationships and leave aside the question of whether they are intended or not. In fact, only action can be intended; causal relationships cannot be intended. The main difficulty in using this terminology lies in determining who recognizes the causal relationships and who does not. The real magnitude of the problem can be seen if we ask the question, does anyone really comprehend or recognize the causal relationships in sociology? Perhaps the sociologist is more sophisticated than the layman, but it seems that the really large class of causal relationships is not recognized by either.

Some causal relationships are believed in by the general public, and some other causal relationships are believed in by experts; but the experts are not unanimous in their beliefs. Merton's essay on the self-fulfilling prophecy is quite appropriately considered at this point. He quotes Thomas, "If men define situations as real, they are real in their consequences" (Merton, 1949). In other words, if men believe they understand causal relationships, they will act accordingly.

These perceived or recognized causal relationships need not be in error. But there are certain processes involved that tend to complicate Thomas's statement. The recognition of existing causal relationships can lead to the formation of novel causal relationships. Electronically minded sociologists choose to call this process feedback. Simon discusses the question in the form of the consequences of a correct social prediction (Simon, 1957). A trivial example would be the following: I go to lunch at noon, but I see that everyone else goes to lunch at noon, and therefore I have to wait in line. The next day I go to lunch ten minutes earlier, but most of the others have made the same decision I did, so that we still have to wait in line. In general, social life more closely resembles the croquet game in *Alice in Wonderland* than it resembles a biological organism.

Suppose we made a distinction between those causal relationships that are the direct recognized consequences of purposive action and those that are only indirectly related to these social-psychological processes. We might choose to think of the former as manifest in Merton's sense, while the latter is latent, for an unrecognized causal relationship cannot be the basis of intentional or purposive action. An example will reveal the main difficulty of this distinction. Let us suppose that prior to Malthus' *Essay* the general public did not recognize the relationship

29

between the number of children in each family and population pressure on resources. Then indirect (unrecognized) causal relationships falling within the sphere of ecology should be examined. But since Malthus wrote, public officials have become aware of this relationship between family size and population pressure and now seek to control it as a matter of policy. The relationship is no longer an indirect one, and therefore we must supplement ecology with social psychology and political science to explain it. In fact, one of the safest predictions in social science is that the effort to bring such indirect relationship under control will continue.

We can now relate functionalism to ecology. Human ecologists examine the reciprocal relationships between resources and social organization. In doing so, they consider indirect social relationships, that is, aggregate phenomena rather than social-psychological phenomena. The risks that ecologists run because of exclusion of social-psychological considerations are suggested in the Malthusian example above. Functionalists examine the indirect causal relationships that link elements or parts of structure. They also consider the causal implications of structure for the social-psychological sphere as in Merton's essay on social structure and anomie (Merton, 1949). We may preserve the functionalist terminology if we define a functional relationship as an indirect causal relationship in which structure is the antecedent condition, or cause, while either structure or behavior is a consequence, or effect. These two types of relationship could be distinguished but need not be in this study.

Both ecology and functionalism are concerned with the indirect causal relationships involved in human aggregates. They both seek to explain regularities revealed by human behavior in the aggregate rather than the behavior of individual humans.

The theorists of both ecology and functionalism, however, ignore the effect of social-psychological processes upon aggregate relationships. For some problems, the social-psychological proces-

30

ses can be safely ignored; for others, it is less wise. Six possible effects can be sketched out.

Consider the effects of social-psychological processes upon aggregate relationships. Some actions are generally recognized as affecting aggregate relationships; some actions affect aggregate relationships but no one is aware of it; and some actions do not affect aggregate relationships.

Now consider the effects of aggregate relationships, or processes. Some aggregate relationships may affect other aggregate relationships; some aggregate relationships may have an unrecognized effect upon social-psychological processes and some aggregate relationships may have a recognized effect upon social-psychological processes.

The fourth possibility is contained in Durkheim's insistence upon social facts as explanations for other social facts. The fifth possibility is suggestive of Durkheim's analysis of suicide, for he takes individual actions, cumulates them to obtain rates in terms of social aggregates, and then develops an aggregate explanation for variations among the rates.

At this point, we are ready to attempt further conceptualization. We have seen some of the relationships between ecology and functionalism, but we still need a scheme that encompasses both, for the relationship between residential areas and social structure cuts across the two systems.

The relationship we wish to examine between residential areas and social structure already can be stated somewhat more precisely. First, we intend to examine the consequences of social structure for the characteristics of residential areas. Secondly, given the characteristics of residential areas, we shall examine the influence of location or space upon social behavior, social structure, and culture.

The first task can be handled adequately with the conceptual apparatus already developed. The second task, however, requires that a minimal amount of psychology be imbedded in any aggregate theory.

31

The approach to the problem under consideration that we shall develop begins with a simple decision model and then of necessity proceeds to complicate it with aggregate considerations. A "decision" is defined as a choice among alternatives. The alternatives and their objective consequences may be regarded as information, while the criteria for choosing among the alternatives may be regarded as values. Any particular decision, then, is a function of the values and information available to a given individual at a given time. Both values and information are communicated to individuals. We may think of the communication as passing through social channels. These social channels are to a large extent determined by social structure.

By defining decision in this way, it will be possible to shift attention from the specific psychological content of the act of decision-making to the relationship between the resulting choice and aggregate social phenomena. We will be interested in cases in which the subject is not self-consciously aware of his decision as well as those cases in which the subject is self-conciously aware of his alternatives, their consequences, and his own values. The failure of an individual to recognize alternatives or consequences as they appear to others will suggest special problems of analysis rather than the absence of a decision. This model explicitly contains constraints upon the individual decision-maker that may be used for aggregate predictions. Major attention is focused upon the constraints implicit in communication processes, especially the socialization process.

The decision process itself can take on quite different forms. The greatest differences among the forms of decision may be expressed in different modes of orientation. Lesser variations may be expressed within each mode of orientation.

The purposive-rational mode of orientation contains the main features that are included in the usual decision theories, or theories of rational behavior. The individual explicitly lists alternatives and their consequences, explicitly states a criterion, compares the consequences to his criterion, and thereby selects

32

a course of action, or makes a decision. The values, or criteria by which selection is guided, may vary widely. Some of the possibilities would include financial profit, social prestige, power, or psychological security. In empirical situations, several values may be competing; appropriate mathematical decision models are only beginning to appear.

Other modes of orientation are not so simply related to the usual decision theories. The *traditional* mode of orientation does not contain the highly individualistic decision processes of the purposive-rational mode. In the traditional mode, an individual may present alternatives to a source of authority, such as village elder or sacred book. He then abides by the decision of this authority. Some writers even envisage a completely integrated culture that prestructures decisions for individuals by presenting them with only one alternative at each point of choice. In this view, everyone is socialized into habitual behavior as in Durkheim's notion of mechanical solidarity.

Another important mode of orientation, infrequently investigated, is the short-run hedonistic, or undeferred gratification, mode, often imputed to America's urban lower classes. Here the listing of alternatives and the computation of consequences assumes a peculiarly truncated form. The purposive element is absent in the sense that explicit future expectations play a negligible role in decision making.

Other modes of orientation could be considered. The main purpose of the modes is to express types of decision processes that have been excluded from the usual theories of rational behavior. The view taken here is that much of the behavior classified as nonlogical or irrational need not be so regarded. So long as the individual is consistent with his own mode of orientation, he is rational in terms of that mode. It is the job of the theorist to describe each mode of orientation, not to express his ethical views as to which one is best. Too often rational means good in the language of social science.

The frame of reference of an individual may be regarded as a mode of orientation if it is shared by a number of people. We shall assume that modes of orientation can be communicated. We will exclude the idiosyncratic syndromes of the mentally ill from modes of orientation, but those aspects of character structure that are socially transmitted will be considered. Thus, we will, in effect, focus our attention upon social processes.

Modes of orientation, as used here, need not be uniform throughout a cultural system. Usually several modes will be found within a given culture. Further, most individuals will not consistently act toward all objects with a single mode of orientation. However, for the concept to be useful, they must consistently act with one mode toward a designated class of objects. To illustrate, we can think of two classes of objects, sacred and secular. Both classes are found in a single culture, and individuals are capable of acting appropriately toward both.

The environmental system, the cultural system, social organization, and social structure all have consequences for the decision process. All affect the formation of channels for communication of values and information. The cultural system itself consists of the content that is communicated. But the information may be partially determined by the environment, social structure, or social organization. When we say that aggregate phenomena serve as limiting factors upon social-psychological processes, we mean in part that they limit the alternatives and consequences that can be presented to an individual.

We now have a sufficient conceptual apparatus to proceed to more direct analysis of our problem. The relationships between social structure and residential area can be expressed in the terminology now available to us. The distinction between ecology and functionalism at a theoretical level is no longer an obstacle and empirical materials gathered in terms of either conceptual scheme can be utilized in the remainder of this essay.

3

Urban Social Structure

WHAT is urban social structure? Indeed, is there a distinctively urban social structure? Preliminary answers will be given in this chapter.

Social structure has already been defined as a set of persistent patterned social relationships among persons or positions. The subclass of social structure, social stratification, can be defined precisely in these terms. If a ranking system among the participants in the social relationships can be delineated, then that ranking system, if its has behavioral consequences, will be called a stratification system whether the consequences are recognized by

35

the participants or not. A ranking system exists among any kind of units if a relationship of inequality exists among the units with respect to some characteristic. We shall assume that the relationship of inequality is recognized by the participants.

Delineation of a stratification system consists of two tasks. First, the characteristics upon which the ranks are based should be ascertained. These characteristics may be quite numerous, and they may not be related one to another in simple ways. Second, the existence of boundaries among groups of participants with respect to the ranking system can be investigated. These boundaries may be established with respect to several criteria and the boundary for one criterion may not coincide with the boundary for another criterion. These boundaries are usually treated as defining social classes or castes.

The basis for much American social-stratification literature stems from a consideration of the fact that ranking with respect to many different attributes yields essentially the same ordering of persons in American society. Direct measures of ranking include the objective indicators of education, income, and occupation, the reputational indicators as developed in a sociometric type of interview, the cultural or style of life symbolic indicators of values such as consumers goods, and subjective psychological identification with classes as determined by interview.

The characteristics of boundaries within the American stratification system have been the source of much controversy. This controversy can be most readily traced to the ideological concerns of different scholars, although the empirical data are themselves sufficiently inconsistent to lead to much debate. Boundaries may be established with respect to any of the direct measures of ranking. Discontinuities in the distribution of objective characteristics, discontinuities as revealed in the judgments of individuals, and the phenomenon of mobility of persons with respect to a ranking system may be criteria for boundaries. The number and characteristics of boundaries in the American stratification system have tended to differ among the several research methods, as well as among users of these methods (Kahl, 1957).

A crucial difficulty in stratification theory already has been implied by this discussion. Not only do different investigators find different systems of stratification in America, but evidently different participants in the system have different views of it. Some of these differences in view can be accounted for by the different positions a person may have in the stratification system. Nevertheless, we must face up to the possibility that there is no such thing as a stratification system in the sense usually implied in sociology. For the usual treatment assumes the existence of a single, definite unidimensional hierarchy that everyone is more or less aware of and abides by. The barnyard pecking order is the usual sociological model.

The problem may be illustrated by reference to the story of the blind men and the elephant. Recall that each blind man grasped the elephant by a different part, and therefore each described the elephant differently. They were describing a common phenomenon from different vantage points. But the common phenomenon, the elephant, was a concrete entity in its own right. A social-stratification system is not a concrete entity in the same sense. The stratification system ultimately is a model that the investigator imposes upon the concrete data. But the data from which the model is inferred need not be a concrete hierarchical system in their own right. More likely the concrete data of concern are themselves the differing descriptions of the phenomenon (Levi-Strauss, 1953).

This view is borrowed from Leach's argument in *Political Systems of Highland Burma* (1954). Leach notes varying points of view among the Kachins of the Burma Hills as to what their political structure actually is. Further, he notes that although the Kachin political theory appears to be expressed in a rigid and inflexible manner, the actualities reflect a loose and rapidly shifting situation. In part, Leach attributes the rigid interpreta-

37

tion by anthropologists to the Western mind with its emphasis upon neat and tidy classifications. More important, however, is the possibility that the inconsistencies among points of view are clues to the essential features of the political structure.

The lesson to be learned is this. Instead of averaging the various points of view to a single social structure, and regarding deviation from this single structure as either random error or pure ignorance, one can examine the apparent inconsistencies as clues to underlying regularities. These underlying regularities, however, may lead to a dynamic model predictive of change. The sources of tension can become the focus of analysis rather than the sources of agreement.

Leach contrasts his own point of view with that of the structure-function school of thought. Perhaps a long quotation will clarify this point.

English social anthropologists have tended to borrow their primary concepts from Durkheim rather than from either Pareto or Max Weber. Consequently they are strongly prejudiced in favour of societies which show symptoms of "functional integration," "social solidarity," "cultural uniformity," "structural equilibrium." Such societies, which might well be regarded as moribund by historians or political scientists, are commonly looked upon by social anthropologists as healthy and ideally fortunate. Societies which display symptoms of faction and internal conflict leading to rapid change are on the other hand suspected of "anomie" and pathological decay. . . . The social anthropologist normally studies the population of a particular place at a particular point in time and does not concern himself greatly with whether or not the same locality is likely to be studied again by other anthropologists at a later date. . . . When anthropological societies are lifted out of time and space in this way the interpretation that is given to the material is necessarily an equilibrium analysis, for if it were not so, it would certainly appear to the reader that the analysis was incomplete. But more than that, since, in most cases, the research work has been carried out once and for all without any notion of repetition, the presentation is one of *stable* equilibrium; the authors write as if the Trobrianders, the Tikopia, the

38

Nuer are as they are, now and for ever. . . . When the anthropologist attempts to describe a social system he necessarily describes only a model of the social reality. This model represents in effect the anthropologist's hypothesis about "how the social system works." The different parts of the model system therefore necessarily form a coherent whole—it is a system in equilibrium. But this does not imply that the social reality forms a coherent whole; on the contrary the reality situation is in most cases full of inconsistencies: and it is precisely these inconsistencies which can provide us with an understanding of the process of social change (Leach, 1954, pp. 7–8).

In particular, Leach has Radcliffe-Brown in mind as a follower of Durkheim. Both Leach and Levi-Strauss criticize Radcliffe-Brown's definition of social structure as the complex network of actually existing social relationships. They state that such a definition of social structure is too concrete, that it does not take cognizance of social structure as a model. The difference between these two points of view may be resolved by noting that Radcliffe-Brown has a descriptive notion of social structure; whereas Leach and Levi-Strauss seek to explain social structure through model construction. The data of social structure throughout this study are identical with those implied by Radcliffe-Borwn's definition, but the further need for a dynamic explanatory model for these data is also recognized.

The traditional sociological literature is relevant to urban social structure. Little specific attention has been paid to the city itself, but the omission is symptomatic of the difficulties lying ahead. In general, the nineteenth-century sociologists took a macroscopic point of view and described the social structure of whole societies as revealed by historical data. Recent sociologists, however, have more often dealt with the social structure of small, self-contained communities as revealed by interview and systematic observation. Most recent work falls into a microscopic point of view, save for several major nationwide surveys of opinions. In either case, most of the literature is either too broad or too restricted to enable us to focus on urban social structure directly. On the whole, stratification has been given the major emphasis in recent discussions of social structure and will be examined most carefully here.

The macroscopic view of social structure viewed historically is a descendant of Marx's theories of social and economic organization. Marx tended to reduce most aspects of stratification to the economic basis of class; the fundamental distinction lies in whether one is bourgeois or proletarian, that is, in one's relationship to the means of production. All of his structural concepts are organized around this distinction. The bourgeois control of economic matters implies bourgeois control of political matters. Further, all functional consequences of structure are implied by the economic organization of society—namely, the capitalist society in which such a distinction exists—and by the inevitable conflict between classes, which, coupled with the concepts of class consciousness and solidarity, provides a social psychology of social relationships. Thus, the Marxian synthesis relates stratification to economic structure and power structure, states the functions of stratification, and contains a social psychology of stratification. Much subsequent sociological writing has tended away from this synthetic view.

The critics of Marx, such as Pareto, Durkheim, and Weber retained broad syntheses in their own formulations of social structure (Parsons, 1949). For example, Pareto's cyclical theory of history based on notions of circulation of elites and of fundamental, slowly changing residues is a direct attack upon Marx's view of social change; Pareto considers alternative functions for stratification and an alternative social psychology. Weber decomposed stratification into class, status, and party, yet he accepted the obligation to state the relationships among these components. Durkheim attempted to escape from the obligation of a social psychology, yet his analysis of the division of labor

40

ranges from ecological and demographic considerations on one hand to the relationship between normative integration and psychological integration on the other.

But most recent macroscopic endeavors have come to regard stratification as a thing apart from social structure, with correlates instead of functions, and with few social-psychological aspects. Current interest is focused upon describing multiple dimensions of social structure but often without reference to a larger synthetic context of theory and analysis.

Seven specific criticisms of contemporary macroscopic theory will be considered here:

First, stratification is abstracted from other structural concepts. The relationship between culture and stratification has been reduced to a descriptive listing of the different customs that are found in different social classes. Even the relationship between the ethnic group and the social class is considered only in a restricted sense. To sum up, stratification has been posed as a special topic of inquiry that can be pursued in a vacuum; stratification can be defined and measured independently of other social concepts. Much technical progress in scale construction has been made within this narrow conception but little theoretical interpretation of the results is possible.

Second, the functions of stratification have been neglected, as is already implied in the first criticism. Not merely have the relationships among structural elements been neglected but the processes that underlie these relationships have been largely ignored. Stratification has been investigated as a self-perpetuating mechanism, as in Hollingshead's *Elmtown's Youth,* but little light has been thrown upon the more general consequences of these processes (Hollingshead, 1949). The need for dynamic models is indicated by these omissions.

Third, survey methods and data have been emphasized while historical and anthropological data have been neglected. Perhaps this point accounts for the first two, for the survey method tends

41

to tear data out of context unless it is skillfully employed. Structure is not easily inferred from the responses of individuals. Context or structural considerations must be imposed during the survey design or it will never enter the study.

Fourth, prestige ranking has been considered a sufficient objective of stratification studies. The Warner studies (Warner and Lunt, 1941; Warner *et al.,* 1949) and the North-Hatt study (North and Hatt, 1947) are specific examples, but this tendency is visible in most of the other studies in the 1930's and 1940's. A literature in power structure has been inspired by Hunter's research (Hunter, 1953) and Mills' writing (Mills, 1946); while Centers (Centers, 1949) investigated psychological indentification and social class. However these are recent and as yet tangential developments in the stratification literature. What are the functions, or consequences, of high prestige? The listing of correlates at one point in time will not do as an answer to this question.

Fifth, some sort of "mass" society concept is apparently needed for the macroscopic view of stratification. Ranking seems to exist as an abstract property of society completely apart from concrete social relationships and devoid of psychological content. Theoretical discussion by Davis and Moore (Davis and Moore, 1945) has stressed a relationship between ranking and the division of labor by applying an economic analogy of the scarcity of commodities to the sociological problem of the allocation of positions in society, as brought out by Simpson (Simpson, 1956). However, this argument does not explicitly delve into concrete social relationships. The social-psychological aspects of social relationships are largely neglected. Clearly, Radcliffe-Brown's view of social structure retains social-psychological elements in social structure, and unless we can demonstrate empirically that all social relationships are impersonal or anonymous, we had better include social psychology in our theories.

Sixth, no locale nexus for social relationships is provided by this macroscopic view of stratification. Some stability of actors and interactions in a social system is necessary before social relationships can be said to exist. Although stability of inter-action can be conceived of without reference to any specific locale, most stable interactions do take place within a specific locale, and the characteristics of the locale influence the char-acteristics of the interaction.

Seventh, the macroscopic view ignores the variations in strati-fication within society—variations among regions, among subcul-tures, between rural and urban areas, and even within social strata. Perhaps references to a single system of stratification in the United States are valid when crude comparisons with rather different stratification systems are intended; otherwise the notion of a single stratification system in the United States is likely to be misleading. True, if mass culture has an extreme homogeniz-ing influence upon the United States, then this objection will no longer hold. But as yet the internal variations are quite striking.

Let us turn to the microscopic approach to social structure. This approach tends to be more concrete than the macroscopic one. Radcliffe-Brown's conception of social structure and social relations is typically concrete. The field methods employed in the analysis of these kinds of social relations permit direct observa-tion of the social relationship. Weber's conception of a social relationship as existing in the probability that individuals act toward each other in characteristic ways is quite close to Rad-cliffe-Brown's concern with empirical regularities (Weber, 1947).

Radcliffe-Brown also placed a holistic stamp upon the micro-scopic approach, though he recognized that complex modern societies could not readily be studied in these terms. His con-cern for institutional analysis in particular derived from his holistic emphasis. Indeed, within a relatively small, self-con-tained homogeneous society this microscopic approach is actu-ally equivalent to a macroscopic one. However, in larger societies

43

the microscopic approach is not feasible, so that some other approach must be used to study social relationships.

An alternative social-psychological approach defines social structure in terms of role, norm, and expectation. Studies of socialization, conformity, and deviation often employ this terminology (Parsons, 1951). This approach and the previous one may be linked together by the expectations concept. We may define "role" as a set of norms specific to a position, and define "norm" in terms of shared expectations. The shared expectations determine social relationships. Within a particular group we can identify roles with reciprocal social relationships. In this way, one can translate statements about social relationships into statements about roles (Bates, 1956).

Studies of stratification in the United States using a microscopic approach have tended to restrict their scope to prestige ranking, for example, the community studies of the 1930's. Therefore, the functional criticisms of the macroscopic approach also apply to the microscopic approaches. However, anthropological studies of social structure deal with kinship structure and its relationships to other aspects of social structure, thereby escaping these criticisms.

The microscopic approaches assume a common body of actors in mutually meaningful interaction or with stable social relationships among themselves. This assumption is often reasonable for societies with little migration, homogeneous cultures, and little social change. Small numbers of population are implied if the common body of actors, or at least some of them designated as judges, are expected to be in interaction with most of the rest of the population. Most of the specifically anthropological research techniques are feasible only for small populations.

All of the assumptions listed in the previous paragraph are invalid with respect to the urban United States. Of course, the structure of certain parts of a city, as well as the structure of certain cliques in a city, may be examined with these assumptions considered as valid. *Family and Kinship in East London* (Young and Willmott, 1957) illustrates the first kind of study, while Floyd Hunter's *Community Power Structure* illustrates the second (Hunter, 1953). But if there is any single social structure containing all of the inhabitants of the city, it will not be found in this way.

How can the merits of the macroscopic and the microscopic approach be combined? Will such a combination be appropriate to urban social structure? Let us indicate some merits of each approach.

The macroscopic approach can include the insights of historical research and of social anthropology. Both of these bodies of literature are organized around an institutional approach. Historical research stresses the relationship among institutions over great periods of time while social anthropology expresses the relationship among institutions at a particular time as revealed by social relationships. By placing the context of stratification in society as a total system this approach encourages a multifunctional analysis of stratification. Prestige itself is one of the less important aspects of stratification in such an analysis. Power, values, social interests, and economic consequences can all receive greater attention. Indeed, prestige itself can be regarded as a manifestation of values.

Some deficiencies of the macroscopic approach stem from the lack of information on concrete social relationships obtained in empirical research in large heterogeneous social units. Once the anthropological methods break down one is left mainly with demographic and historical data. Neither of these kinds of data is easily related to the specific structures and specific behavioral systems that we would like to analyze in our society. The survey method as yet has not been used with such formulations. The survey measures individual responses directly, not social structure. The mechanism of reference groups may be employed to

45

relate individual responses to social or demographic categories, but this device still does not yield direct evidence about social relationships, only evidence of identification.

The microscopic approaches have desirable properties for empirical research, but, save for the anthropological approach, they have not developed equally significant theory. Role, norm, deviation, expectation, and sanction must be placed within a broader context of social structure before they enable us to analyze any large heterogeneous social units. These concepts have, for the most part, been used descriptively. Empirical research in small communities has tended to be highly community specific, that is, the man is ranked in terms of a local interaction system but the implications for his rank in some other community are not investigated, and therefore we cannot generalize the results.

Next let us consider the main problems presented by urban social structure:

First, limitations of time alone suggest that close personal relationships cannot be established and maintained among all the inhabitants of a city. Impersonal relationships may be numerous among those people involved in many interactions. In brief casual contacts between persons only superficial information can be communicated, yet this kind of information will commonly be the basis for evaluating and ranking them. Reliance upon symbols to communicate this information leads to a certain standardization of ranking criteria within impersonal relationships. Address, car, dress, speech, and manners as symbols become important criteria. Of course, within personal relationships, the esteem of role performance (Davis, 1948, pp. 93–94) and the repute of personal evaluations (Gordon, 1959, pp. 245–46) will still be found. Nevertheless, if we are to refer to a reputational stratification system for the entire city, we will probably have to describe the system in terms of highly visible, standardized symbols. These symbols do not communicate the type of evaluations implied by esteem or repute.

Second, the degree of cultural homogeneity and the extent to which channels of communication link together the various groups in the population affect the extent to which an over-all stratification system can be described. The existence of subcultures, which may or may not follow the boundary lines of the stratification system, tends to obliterate any precise over-all ranking system. While some subcultures may be ranked as aggregates in a crude way, comparisons between any two persons in two different subcultures may have little meaning.

Third, the stability of the population of a city affects the extent to which a stratification system can be described. Newcomers are only slowly absorbed into the existing network of social relationships that anthropologists seek to describe. Rapid social change engendered by rapid technological change serves as a stimulus to population movement and to the development of new occupations, which cannot readily be interpreted in terms of a previous stratification system. Thus, the economic system, as the source of technological change, may lead to flexibility or blurring in an over-all stratification system.

The movement of population confronts us with further problems of similarities among the social structures of different cities. If a family moves, how is it placed in the new stratification system? Are characteristics such as size of city or economic base of city crucial in this problem? To what extent is there a national stratification system that can guide us to an answer to this question? These questions must be dealt with before we can speak of a characteristic urban social structure, as opposed to the social structure of specific cities. The heterogeneity of values within a city has already posed difficulties for us; now we must deal with the heterogeneity of values on a national level as well. For the newcomer must necessarily be judged by superficial symbols, and the meanings attached to these symbols can be similar only if the systems of values in the various cities are similar.

To this point numerous difficulties have been indicated in any attempt to create a satisfactory schematization of urban social structure. Let us now sketch out a possible solution to these problems. There are undoubtedly several systems of social structure within each city. Of these, two must be distinguished now. We may refer to the over-all system of superficial symbols used to rank persons in a city as the "urban stratification system." This is the only system that is shared by the inhabitants of the city and participated in by most members of the city. The system can be described in terms of prestige, though the significance of the system is by no means summarized in these terms.

We may also think of the city as composed of numerous subcultures, some following social class lines and some following racial or ethnic lines as well as others. Within the subcultures, the urban stratification system will be recognized, but it will not be regarded in the same way in the different groups. In general, those persons in an advantageous position in the system will tend to sanctify the system and argue for the status quo. Those not so fortunate will take a different view.

These two systems of social structure may be studied by different research methods. The urban stratification system may be directly measured by survey techniques. The abstractness of the survey technique will not be harmful, since a symbolic system is under investigation not relationships among persons. The urban subcultural system may be studied directly by anthropological techniques. Data pertinent to both systems will be found in the census tract tabulations. If surveys measure the different views of the over-all stratification system held within the different subcultures then these two systems can be linked.

We have, then, an abstract, over-all system and a set of concrete subsystems. We may borrow Leach's model for the analysis of the subsystems in their relationship to the over-all system: The differential meaning and value placed on the over-all system within the subsystems can be used to construct a dynamic model of social stratification. This dynamic model should express the processes by which the over-all stratification is maintained as well as the processes that tend toward making changes in the system.

Within the subcultures we can investigate concrete social relationships. The esteem of role performance and the repute of personal evaluations will be pertinent here. While esteem will be involved in all performances of roles, the most important situation for heads of household will be found in work, with family roles almost as important. Thus, the knowledge of esteem will generally be restricted to rather small, but perhaps highly stable, social systems. Similarly, the knowledge of repute will be re-restricted to family, peer groups, and others within primary social relationships. The social systems in which esteem and repute are operative will ordinarily be much smaller than subcultures. Systems of repute will tend to be entirely within single subcultures, but systems of esteem may cross subcultural boundaries.

The existence and the meaningfulness of esteem and repute in the urban setting may be challenged from two points of view. First, the amount of mobility, previously mentioned, will tend to disrupt the establishment of primary or close social relationships within which these concepts are meaningful. Second, the existence of social disorganization, or anomie, within a subculture would have the same disruptive effect. This possibility has been suggested for the lower classes in general and the recent migrants to the city in particular, especially those migrants marked out by ethnic or racial distinctions.

Recent research, however, indicates that greater stability of social relationships exists in the city than had been previously believed. In particular, the importance of kinship ties among those groups formerly believed to be disorganized has been emphasized. Although esteem and repute probably may not have the same significance in urban social structure that they have in a small, stable community, they may have more significance than the classical treatment of urban social structure suggests.

The over-all urban stratification system may also be interpreted in social-psychological terms. The concept of *social distance* (Bogardus, 1928) may be used to express prestige ranking as it affects social relationships concretely. Social distance need not be restricted to the social relationships among racial and ethnic groups but may be used to describe relationships among social classes, occupational groups, or any other grouping. Social distance may be measured behaviorally—who marries whom, who lives near whom, and so forth; or it may be measured psychologically by the traditional social-distance scale in which persons are asked to rank various ethnic and racial groups according to a series of hypothetical social relationships—would you marry an X, eat meals with an X, have an X in your neighborhood, in your school, at your job, and so forth.

Social distance is a useful concept because it describes an aspect of interaction that can take place within any social relationship and it also describes this interaction in terms of participation in different institutional settings. These merits can be retained in the generalized view which we are taking. Although social distance has been traditionally associated with caste distinctions, the inclusion of social classes on a social-distance scale should also prove illuminating. The occupations that North and Hatt ranked by prestige might be ranked on a social-distance scale as well as the social-class categories of Centers. A comparison between these rankings and those of various racial and ethnic groupings should be illuminating. In particular, occupational, ethnic, and racial combinations should be ranked (such as Negro doctor) in order to determine the relative importance of each component in assigning social distance. By this approach, the survey technique can help us to describe the over-all stratification system in terms that will simplify the further study of subcultures. The determination of boundaries in a stratification system is especially aided by social-distance measures. The fact that much behavior in specific situations cannot be predicted from knowledge of the symbolic aspects of stratification does not detract from the significance of this approach.

So far we have included elements of both macroscopic and microscopic approaches to social stratification and have begun to delineate a dynamic model for explaining over-all patterns of stratification. The criticisms of the macroscopic approach as lacking social-psychological context are met by the inclusion of elements from both approaches in the system model. The main criticism of the microscopic approach, its lack of applicability, is also met. But the functional criticisms of the current macroscopic approach as lacking economic and political relevance deserve more attention.

The total effect of the functional criticisms is to call attention to the narrow focus on prestige ranking in recent work. The general institutional, structural, or functional context of stratification has been neglected. But how does the approach described above escape these criticisms?

We must sketch out the institutional context of stratification before we can answer this question. Let us consider first the economic system, the political system, and the cultural system.

The economic system has been correctly emphasized in the stratification literature. The dominance of economic institutions in the culture of the West, and especially of the United States, is sufficient to justify this emphasis. But the relationship between the economic system and the stratification system is not so simple. The over-all stratification system is based on symbols. Weber's notion of status as "style of life" (Weber, 1946) and Veblen's notions of invidious distinction and conspicuous consumption (Veblen, 1931) represent similar conceptions of stratification.

51

Some symbols cost money and are therefore restricted to those persons who can afford them; other symbols, however, stand for the person's position in the productive processes, specifically his occupation; still other symbols denote racial or ethnic position.

Various empirical studies have underscored the importance of occupation in predicting prestige ranking in the United States. Since symbols reflect values we may note that such intrinsic characteristics of occupation as skill and responsibility relate to the prestige system more closely than do the extrinsic rewards. (Barber, 1957). Thus, the significance of position in the productive processes is not solely a matter of financial return but reflects more general cultural evaluations.

We have already noted that economic processes related to technological change can result in a shifting occupational structure, and therefore in a shifting stratification system. We may further note that the organization of economic activities into firms or bureaucracies affects the occupational system and stratification system. Such popular works as *The Organization Man* (Whyte, 1957) dwell on the rigidifying effects of bureaucracy upon stratification. In particular, the reliance upon academic degrees for entrance into the management hierarchy may increase the rigidity of stratification or the presence of boundaries.

The development of labor unions as counters to the power of management further affects the stratification system. Paradoxically, the pooling of the economic interests of workers in unions has not led to generalized class conflict. The ultimate effects of unionization upon the rigidifying tendencies of class is by no means clear.

In summary, the relationship between the economic system and the stratification system is as follows. Many consequences for the stratification system stem from the economic system. However, these economic consequences in no sense entirely define or determine the stratification system. Many other factors affect stratification including those self-maintaining factors found within stratification. Any predictions as to the future state of the stratification system must take account of economic factors, but these economic factors are not sufficient to allow prediction by themselves.

The specific relationship between the economic system and the social structure of a particular city is not simple. When a single, locally owned industrial concern dominates the economy of a small city, then the patriarchal, not to say feudal, effects upon the social structure will be quite clear. In Elmtown, for example, approximately thirty-five per cent of the adult males were employed by one locally owned industrial concern (Warner, *et al.*, 1949, pp. 101–114). Of course, the textile-mill towns of New England and the South are extreme examples of this situation. But when the economic base of the community is more diversified, the effects upon the stratification system are not so clear. Possibly a white-collar city, such as Washington, D.C., would tend toward a system different from an industrial city. In fact, social structure must reflect economic variations of place as well as economic variations of time if there are any economic effects at all.

When we turn to the political system quite a different set of problems awaits us. Although the prestige ranking system contains some hints as to the over-all distribution of power in society, the actual controls of power are invested in large organizations. For the most part, he who has power in our society is he who has a strategic position in a giant organization, be it political, military, industrial, labor union, or whatnot. Therefore, many high ranking persons, such as those in the medical profession, may have little power (save through their own mass organization, the A.M.A.) while some low ranking persons may have considerable power. The American political system, national and local, is a mediator between the conflicts and pressures of numerous organizations; therefore control over these organizations provides access to power.

The maintenance of over-all power relations, however, has a good deal to do with stratification. In our democratic system, voting has very definite long-run effects upon the over-all structure of power relations. But the phenomenon of voting itself is greatly affected by the stratification system, as shown by numerous studies of voting behavior (Lipset, 1960).

On the other hand, the effects of power upon the stratification system are less clear. Certainly, shifts in the power structure will affect the stratification system; certainly, rigidity of the power structure will also affect the stratification system, as suggested by the position of the Negro in the North and South. But there is no objectively visible link, such as occupation, in relation to the economic system, through which we can establish these connections. In part, the phenomenon of power thrives on secrecy, the data are not available. But in part also, the relationship may simply not be as close as that between the economic system and the stratification system. The study of power should focus more closely upon the relations between large organizations than upon stratification.

Within a particular city there may be an informal power structure presiding over community-wide decisions, especially those of a community welfare nature. This power structure wields decisive influence when a project requiring volunteer financing is involved, for the persons in the controlling positions are those who normally provide large lump sums. Hunter's examples of decisions in *Community Power Structure* are mainly of this sort, so that the degree of control over other community activities is less clear. In *Middletown*, the Lynds found a more stringent control wielded by the power structure, but the size of community and dominance of a single, locally owned industry account in part for the difference (Lynd and Lynd, 1929).

When we turn to the relationship between the stratification system and the system of symbols and values, we are really dealing with the internal mechanisms of the stratification system itself. For the over-all stratification system consists of symbols,

54

not persons, and the symbols reflect the values of society. Thus, the definition of a stratification system is dependent upon a certain minimum of common values. The persistence of the stratification system therefore depends upon the communication of these values to subsequent generations.

Suppose we turn to the further question, what are the consequences of the ranking system for behavior? While some of the symbols, such as occupation, represent activities, we can still ask, is the ranking system merely an ordering of behavioral differences, or does the ranking system itself affect behavior? By our definitions, the ranking system must affect behavior to be a stratification system. But how are these consequences expressed?

The most direct answer involves values and information. Different values are found among the different subcultures. These values govern the ways in which the persons in subcultures act toward one another—that is, the social relationships between persons in different subcultures, which leads us back to the initial definition of social structure. The symbolic information permits individuals to perceive the rank and then act according to values. Now, the stratification system must explain not merely the existence of social relationships among subcultures but also the persistence of these social relationships. Thus, the communication of values to subsequent generations must be bounded so that the subcultures themselves persist. The stratification system, by affecting social relationships, can affect communication among subcultures and therefore can perpetuate itself.

The view outlined above is essential to the interpretation of the correlates between stratification and behavior that have been reported by the various survey analysts. It is the distribution of values that frequently enables us to interpret stratification theoretically, not the distribution of prestige itself. Clearly, prestige is defined by values, and is itself a value. The "status seekers" are those who emphasize this value in their decision-making.

The socialization process becomes a key process for the maintenance of the stratification system. The crucial boundaries

55

in the maintenance of the stratification system become the boundaries affecting the content of the socialization process, the channels of communication of values to particular subcultures in subsequent generations.

The emphasis upon subculture can be employed in the relating of stratification to racial and ethnic groups. The latter groups often have been treated as subcultures; as such they stand on the same footing as social classes. Many investigators have pointed out that such racial and ethnic subcultures are often concentrated in the lower social strata, especially in their initial period of immigration. The characteristic rise and diffusion of these people throughout the stratification system has been regarded as the outcome of an assimilation process over several generations. The differential success of various groups in rising has been attributed to their different arrival dates and to social distance between these groups and the dominant groups in society. Social distance is expressed in terms of symbolic differentials between these groups. Some authors define ethnic symbols as cultural symbols and racial symbols as biological symbols. Thus, ethnic symbols may be erased by a cultural assimilation process, whereas biological symbols cannot be. In particular, the position of the Negro is partially explained in terms of the biological character of racial symbols (Broom and Selznick, 1955, Chap. XII).

Several community studies have revealed that a stratification system exists within the racial and ethnic groups roughly paralleling the stratification system among the dominant groups. Thus, social distance exists among members of these groups and is organized around the same symbolic referents as are found within the dominant groups. But contrary evidence is presented by William Foote Whyte (Whyte, 1955). The stratification system within ethnic groups may have features quite unlike the system within the dominant groups, especially with respect to the position of racketeers, politicians, entertainers, and so forth.

The importance of subcultures in the present context stems

from two sources. First, they will be regarded as essential elements in a stratification system. Second, they will enable us to construct a dynamic model of social structure in the sense of Leach (See Chapter Seven).

The result of this institutional survey is to define values, symbols, ethnic groups, and racial groups as parts of the stratification system, but to regard economic and power phenomena as external to the stratification system.

Let us relate this discussion to urban social structure. In particular, let us turn our attention to the relationshp between residential area and urban social structure. In doing so we will be concerned more about the social structure of speciflc cities and less about general societal social structure or the related institutional structure.

The residential area of a city is distinctively a part of the city; as occupation, car, or other status symbols are not. As a symbol, the residential area, or address within the residential area, places a person within the context of a particular urban social structure. It is specific to the city in a way that none of the other familiar indexes of social stratification is.

Earlier we noted that mutual social relationships among all persons in a city was an impossibility; indeed, most inhabitants must remain anonymous to any particular inhabitant. But residential areas may be widely known, and their general social characteristics may also be a matter of common knowledge. A survey could easily provide us with relevant information on this point. Certainly, the residential areas and their social positions are far less anonymous than the individuals in the city. It is likely that any one person's social map of the city would reveal his own position, much as the humorous maps entitled "A New Yorker's View of the United States" or "A Bostonian's View of the United States" reflect both geographical and social factors. But the distortion might be only a stretching and shrinking of the residential areas with the essential geographical relations remaining in the same order throughout.

The residential area presumably reflects values in that the residence itself is a consumers' item. More evidence on the relative weight of different aspects of residential area as a factor in the decision to purchase or rent a home is needed to enlighten us on this point. Relative homogeneity of residential areas with respect to social characteristics is assumed in this statement. The residence itself is a more useful index of social stratification than most other consumers' goods; for the residence as symbol has much the same prestige significance throughout the social scale. This is not to say that the meaning of residence is the same at all levels, but that residence itself is a meaningful symbol in prestige terms at all levels. By contrast, the make and model of automobile, while a prominent issue among the lower classes, may be subordinate to housing desires in the restricted budget of the lower white-collar members of the middle class (such as university professors). Most of the symbols of greatest use in differentiating members of the upper classes are inaccessible to, if not invisible to, members of the lower classes. The public character of residence, the necessity of residence, and the high cost of residence, leads to its importance as a symbol of social position.

The usefulness of residential area as a predictor of social characteristics has been attested to by many community studies, and has been given close attention by the Warner group (Warner, Meeker, and Eells, 1949). Indeed, this group has included residential area in its summary index of social class. This index is intended for use in any urban area of the United States. Its validation rests on its relationship to the stratification system that Warner has studied with a reputational interview.

The residential area is also related to subcultures. Data from newly constructed housing projects suggests that spatial location is an important determinant of clique structure. Further, the congregation of various ethnic subcultures in particular areas may have resulted partly from discrimination by the outside world and partly from preference of the insiders, but the fact remains that once they are concentrated in a single area, the spatial proximity can serve to reinforce the characteristics of the subculture. Perhaps the extreme example of proximity reinforcing culture can be found in the old order Amish of Lancaster County, Pennsylvania, in which isolation plays a role as inverse proximity (Kollmorgen, 1943). Maximum proximity among ingroup members plus minimum proximity to outgroup members yields maximum cultural stability if (1) cultural stability is an end of the ingroup culture (2) static environment (3) proximity determines interaction patterns.

Nevertheless, residential area is only tangentially related to many aspects of social structure. We can learn very little about a power structure from residential areas alone. One aspect of the economic system is expressed in land values, but an aspect only distantly related to the industrial system and occupational structure. Even the socialization process, the heart of the stratification system, is not directly revealed in residential area data. Why, then, its importance in this essay?

Two answers can be given. Let us return to the aggregate problem posed in the previous chapter. A central problem of sociology is the description of supra-individual aggregates.

First, while it is true that residential areas reflect only part of social structure, it is also true that if social structure exists as an aggregate, its effects must be revealed in residential areas. While observations on residential areas are not substitutes for observations on individuals in research, the consequences of social structure can be expressed in terms of their effects upon the social characteristics of areas, and these consequences can be tested by observations on residential areas. The reality of social structure is attested to by the fact that social characteristics of residential areas are not randomly distributed, but are clustered in ways that one might readily predict from the discussion earlier in this chapter.

Second, residential area data can reflect aggregate effects as processes. The Chicago school's adaptation of Simmel's social processes has been widely, and correctly, accused of having only descriptive merit (Alihan, 1938). Accommodation, conflict, invasion, succession, these are certainly descriptive terms. But they need not remain so. Imbedded in a theoretical system they can become theoretical concepts. At the same time, such a theoretical system will be process oriented. Dynamic models might explain these residential area processes. The static view of social structure could be supplemented in this way.

In this chapter the theoretical orientation of the book has been presented. Three tasks were undertaken; these were: (1) definitions of concepts, (2) a critique of current theory and research, and (3) a formulation of a synthetic theoretical approach combining elements from diverse traditions. The next three chapters review data relevant to this approach.

4

Historical Processes

THE problem of this chapter is to provide an adequate description of the historical conditions from which American urban social structure emerged. We shall study the characteristics of European social structure, the effects they have had upon the American scene, and their relationship to the ethnic and racial characteristics peculiar to American urban social structure. The social-psychological processes underlying urban social structure will also be discussed.

First, the characteristics of European urban social structure and the conditions responsible for these characteristics must be

61

determined. Attention will then be shifted to the development of American urban social structure and the social-psychological processes responsible for its characteristics.

Two generalizations have been made with respect to the social structure of Western Europe. Sir Henry Maine, in his study of legal structure, stated that there had been an evolution from status to contract in those aspects of law governing the legal relationships among persons (Maine, 1885, pp. 163–165). In ancient law we find that a person's legal relationships to others is a consequence of his hereditary status in society; while in more recent times, we find legal relationships based upon a contract, which both parties enter into.

Marx drew attention to the rise of new economic classes in Europe replacing the social structure of feudal society (Berlin, 1939). He depicted the bourgeoisie, initially the middle-class merchants, as successfully pressing their demands for legal and political recognition in the social order, and thereby destroying the feudal social order. But in the very achievement of their own liberal aims, the bourgeoisie created a new society in which economic position (as defined by the ownership of the means of production) became the basis for social cleavage. For political and legal equality seemed of little help to the worker who must sell his own labor on an open market, a market in which hostile impersonal forces operated to deprive him of his share of the economy. The operation of these economic forces was such as to drive the workers into a self-conscious class, the proletariat. The ensuing struggles between the bourgeoisie and the proletariat, the class conflict, were to become the essential determinant of the form of a newly emerging society. To Marx, of course, this new society had already been revealed; economic inequality would be abolished through common ownership of the means of production.

These two generalizations of Maine and Marx are, to a certain degree, parallel. Maine's statement may be regarded as

62

similar to Marx's description of the rise of the bourgeoisie. Perhaps we can summarize both positions in the following statement: *The bourgeoisie eliminated legal inequality but replaced it with economic inequality.* For Marx, the bourgeoisie simply acted out the implications of underlying economic forces when they did so, yet the summary seems otherwise to be close to his meaning. In the discussion that follows we shall seek to determine the empirical basis for such a generalization.

Note that this generalization is not quite the same as some statements found in contemporary sociology. The terms "class" and "caste" are often used to designate two major types of social structure. These types are, in most discussions, regarded as varying along a continuum of types of social structure from those in which social position is largely determined by personal achievements to those in which social position is ascribed by traditional hereditary considerations—from an open class system to a caste system. It follows from this type of analysis that caste is characteristic of traditional societies in which social change is imperceptible, and that class is characteristic of industrial society in which social change is endemic. But this analysis is inadequate. First, if Marx had any insight at all, the possibility exists that hereditary lines of class structure of the most rigid type can develop in industrial society. Specifically, the Marxian analysis admits the possibility of the small entrepreneur falling *from* the bourgeois class; but it does not allow for the rise of anyone. Second, other caste elements are entirely neglected in such an analysis. The ritual expression of social distance, the relationship between social structure and religion, the relationship between social structure and power, the intricate possibilities in the relationship between kinship structure and social structure—all these are ignored in the usual class-caste discussion. At most, only the first two elements in this list are considered, and then in a cursory fashion. The discussion to follow will attempt to correct these errors.

The contribution of the Reformation to the present-day middle-class institutions has been drawn to the attention of most sociologists by Weber's essay, *The Protestant Ethic and the Spirit of Capitalism* (Weber, 1930). The contributions of the Middle Ages to middle-class institutions are less well known to sociologists. Therefore, we shall discuss these medieval contributions in some detail.

The rebirth of commerce and the rise of the merchant class in western Europe accompanied the development of novel political, social, and economic institutions in the cities. These institutions tended toward egalitarian legal and political forms; they were accompanied by a democratic political theory extending even to the Conciliar movement within the medieval church, and they could aptly be described as a form of limited democracy in practice (Figgis, 1956, p. 31). To accurately describe these institutions first requires a contrast with the previous urban institutional structure.

The recent descriptions of the preindustrial city by Kingsley Davis (Davis and Golden, 1954) and by Sjoberg (Sjoberg, 1959) complement the historical analysis of Pirenne (Pirenne, 1956), Weber (Weber, 1958), and Maine. An emphasis upon a traditional social structure in such cities maintained by an interpenetration of kinship structure, power structure, and religion is developed by all of these writers. The emphasis upon kinship is articulated in a hereditary tribal or caste system that serves to establish hierarchies of prestige and corresponding hierarchies of political and religious control. The hierarchy of prestige is maintained through myth, ritual, and custom. The combined effect of myth, ritual, and custom is to establish a system of social distance expressed in social interaction, institutional participation (commensalism), and in ideological form. The caste system of India is the extreme type of this social structure.

The existence of fully articulated, kinship-based social sys-

64

tems in large preindustrial cities runs counter to the beliefs of many American urban sociologists. Large population and density are believed to lead to large amounts of interaction among the population and therefore to a decline in ritual expression of social distance among persons resulting finally in the elimination of caste systems. This point of view was most eloquently phrased by Wirth in his essay, "Urbanism as a Way of Life" (Wirth, 1938). Empirical data do not support the argument. Sjoberg's essay "Comparative Urban Sociology" underlines this and other deficiencies in Wirth's position (Sjoberg, 1959).

Special attention must be given to the historical circumstances accompanying the apparent breakdown of caste elements in the urban social structure of western Europe. The peculiar mixture of class and caste elements in American urban social structure can be made clear only with such analysis.

Pirenne attributes the emergence of limited democracy in the medieval city to the needs of the growing merchant class (Pirenne, 1956, pp. 121–50). He sees the demands of the developing middle class as reflected in the needs of an efficient commerce. In particular, a novel legal structure is implied, roughly what Weber referred to as rational-legal, in turn bringing about other institutional shifts (Weber, 1947, pp. 329–333). Pirenne sees the middle-class conflict with the nobility as arising in their demands for limited institutional reform rather than in hostility toward the nobility as a class. Later developments, discussed by Weber (Weber, 1958, pp. 157–196) under the subject of the plebeian city, indicate that the social and political aspirations of the middle classes could lead to the deliberate destruction of the urban nobility as a class.

The evidence supporting these views is drawn from the history of those cities in which commerce earliest became significant both economically and politically, namely the cities of Flanders and the Lombard plain. Other towns and cities showed similar tendencies at a later date; many did not attain the extreme form of urban democracy that we find in the earlier commercial centers. The political innovation of importance was the commune, a body of citizens united by a common oath—the *conjuratio*, to obtain various urban political, economic, and legal reforms. In a large number of instances the commune represented a revolutionary movement. The members of the commune would revolt against the local overlord, often a bishop prior to the settlement of the Investiture Controversy under Innocent III.

The leadership of the commune came from among the wealthier merchants and from the organizations they represented —the guilds. According to Pirenne, these merchants had no definite class origins, but many were probably escaped serfs who attained their freedom originally from the anonymous conditions of travel (Pirenne, 1956, pp. 88–91). In any event, the merchants were external to the hereditary social order, and were necessarily to some extent in conflict with this order. The guild structure, made up of both merchant organizations and craftsman organizations, is a unique development in the western European city. Weber emphasizes that all such organizations in oriental and ancient cities are based on the hereditary social structure, either tribal or caste (Weber, 1958, pp. 201–204). But membership in the medieval guild is based upon occupation alone. The guild seeks to advance the ends of the occupation through various mutual agreements, such as control over resources, production, marketing, training, and recruitment. Thus, we see that both merchant and guild are anachronisms in a traditional social struture. Within the guild and within the commune a theoretical equality of individuals is maintained, expressed in the later Middle Ages by the saying that "city air makes men free," which reflects the statutory provision that if a serf could remain free in a city for a year and a day (or for some other period), the lord had to relinquish his claims over the serf.

The demands of the commune are summarized by Pirenne as follows:

> What they wanted, first of all, was personal liberty, which would assure to the merchant or the artisan the possibility of going and coming, of living where he wished and of putting his own person as well as that of his children under the protection of the seignorial power. Next came the creation of a special tribunal by means of which the burgher would at one stroke escape the multiplicity of jurisdictions to which he was amenable and the inconveniences which the formalistic procedure of ancient law imposed upon his social and economic activity. Then came the instituting in the city of a "peace"—that is to say, of a penal code—which would guarantee security. And then came the abolition of those prestations most incompatible with the carrying on of trade and industry, and with the possession and acquisition of land. What they wanted, in fine, was a more or less extensive degree of political autonomy and local self-government [Prestations are the equivalent of taxes in the feudal system] (Pirenne, 1956, pp. 122–123).

It is quite clear that the merchants intended to establish a privileged middle class rather than to extend the principles of democracy to the entire society. The rural population was explicitly excluded from the newly won privileges of the commune. Political participation within the commune, including the election of its council and the conditions of eligibility to office, was often restricted to property holders. "In the beginning, active membership in the burgher association was bound up with possession of urban land which was inheritable, saleable, exempt from compulsory services and either rent-free or charged only with a fixed amount" (Weber, 1959, p. 118).

The emergence of a novel conception of legal equality, or of legal status, in which hereditary factors play a minimal role accompanies the rise of these urban middle classes. The original claims against the established social structure, the nobility and clergy, while restricted in intent, tend to provide an example for other social strata. The attainment of political power by the *popolo* (a powerful anti-nobility guild-supported confederation within the commune) in Northern Italy further distributed political power among the lower-ranking guilds, especially the artisan guilds. The revolt of the *ciompi* (lowest-ranked guilds and workers) in Florence (in 1378) led to the complete enfranchisement of the medieval artisans for a short period. (Weber, 1958, p. 161; Cheyney, 1936, Chap. IV).

Economic factors, however, are not entirely responsible for the emergence of legal equality in medieval Europe. Weber notes that religious support for the kinship structure ("magical taboo-barriers") in the Orient and in antiquity prohibit the fraternization implicit in Europe in the commune and the *conjuratio*. "The common church which everyone joined in the Middle Ages was absent. . . . Christianity itself was the final element in the destruction of the religious significance of the clans (Weber, 1958, pp. 100, 144, 145). Referring to the family feuds of the early Middle Ages (*Romeo and Juliet*) Weber states:

> Feuds between families raged as violently within as outside the city and many of the oldest civic districts . . . were presumably such areas of feudal power. However, there were no residues —such as were still present in Antiquity—of sacred exclusiveness of families against each other and toward the outside. This was a consequence of the historically memorable precedent in Antioch justly thrust into the foreground by Paul in his letter to the Galatians. There Peter administered the (ritualistic) communal meal to uncircumscribed brethren. Already in the ancient city ritualistic exclusiveness had begun to disappear. The clanless plebs accomplished ritualistic equalization in principle. In the medieval period, chiefly in Central and North European cities, the clans were weak from the beginning and they soon lost all importance as constituencies of the city. Thus the cities became confederations of individual burghers (house owners) (Weber, 1958, p. 98).

The significance of religious factors in the emergence of the *conjuratio* and legal equality is further suggested by the fact that the only group systematically excluded from these privileges was itself religious, namely, the Jews. Weber's proof of this point is contained in the following passage, in which he is contrasting the kinship-based social structure of the Orient and of antiquity with medieval European social structure:

All this was changed in the medieval city, particularly in the North. Here, in new civic creations burghers joined the citizenry as single persons. The oath of citizenship was taken by the individual. Personal membership, not that of kin groups or tribe, in the local association of the city supplied the guarantee of the individual's personal legal position as a burgher.

The North European city often expanded to include not only persons originally foreign to the locality, but merchants foreign to the tribes as well. New civic foundations extended the civic privilege as an attraction to newcomers. To some degree this also occurred incidental to the transformation of older settlements into cities. At times, to be sure, merchants such as are mentioned in Cologne, recruited from the entire circuit of the Occident from Rome to Poland, did not join the local oath-bound urban community, which was founded by the native propertied strata. However, enfranchisement of complete strangers also occurred.

A special position corresponding to that of Asiatic guest people was characteristically occupied in medieval cities only by the Jews. Although in Upper Rhine documents the bishop insists that he called in the Jews "for the greater glory of the city," and though in Cologne shrine-documents the Jews appear as landowners mingling with Christians, ritualistic exclusion of connubialism by the Jews in a manner foreign to the Occident as well as the actual exclusion of table community between Jews and non-Jews and the absence of the Lord's Supper, blocked fraternization. The city church, city saint, participation of the burghers in the Lord's Supper and official church celebrations by the city were all typical of the Occidental cities. Within them Christianity deprived the clan of its last ritualistic importance, for by its very nature the Christian community was a confessional association of believing individuals rather than a ritualistic association of clans. From the beginning, thus, the Jews remained outside the burgher association (Weber, 1958, pp. 102–103).

69

The elimination of legal inequality stemmed from a process which itself had limitations. Eventually, the legal and political institutions of the West came to express these ideas of equality, but the process by which this transpired was uneven and hesitant. The extent to which these developments coincided with middle-class aspirations was a large factor in the ultimate acceptance of these ideas, but also, as in the case of Burke's reaction to the French Revolution, was a factor retarding the extension of these reforms. Similarly, Locke's phrase "life, liberty, and property" captures the spirit of numerous voting restrictions, such as property owning or poll-tax paying.

A similar dualism can be seen in the religious source of equality. The breakdown of hereditary castes was succeeded by religious caste (in the sense of social distance or ritual inequality). The implications of equality in Christianity can be overshadowed by other considerations, as Myrdal was to elucidate in *An American Dilemma* (Myrdal, 1944).

We may now evaluate the first half of our guiding proposition —the bourgeoisie eliminated legal inequality. The current de-emphasis on legal, political, and ritual inequality in the West owes much to the emergence of the middle classes. But religious factors should not be ignored, nor do economic or religious factors have unambiguous implications for equality.

We now turn to the second half of the guiding proposition— the bourgeoisie created economic inequality. In this form the statement is fallacious on two counts. First, economic inequality is found in many societies without a developed middle class. Second, most sophisticated treatments emphasize economic factors in the development of the proletariat beyond the control or even the recognition of the middle classes. We need to show that economic inequality replaced hereditary status inequality as the most important determinant of the social structure, and we need to clarify the part played by the bourgeoisie in this development.

70

In evaluating the factors involved in the development of the modern economic classes, it is of interest to note that the medieval guild, in theory, established economic democracy. The advance from apprentice to journeyman to master was accomplished by a combination of increasing skill and increasing age status. Every guild member had to rise through these ranks; every guild member could, in principle, rise through these ranks. Thus, the theory of the guild specified economic ranks but not economic classes, for individual mobility between ranks was expected.

The breakdown of the guild social order and guild-dominated economy, then, is the first subject for us to discuss (Renard and Weulersse, 1926). The position of the journeyman in the guild could be made worse in two different ways. First, the guild control over economic life could be extended while the criteria for attaining the rank of master were being perverted. The examination of the candidate for master, in particular the qualifications for the masterpiece, could be made so difficult that few journeymen could hope to qualify; sons and sons-in-law of masters, however, might find the examinations less difficult. The outcome of this would be the reduction of the journeymen to serf status, bound by the guild regulations to their master. This possibility was realized in France under the absolute monarchy (ca. 1600–1750). Second, the guild regulations could be swept away entirely, leaving a free market economy to govern the employment of artisan and laborer by entrepreneurs. This possibility was realized in England under the Tudors. Eventually, the guild structure in France followed that of England, yet the intermediate state is of significance in its own right. The existence of class distinction and social distance was an empirical possibility within the guild.

The collapse of guild control was brought about largely through economic factors, but the fact that the Tudor legislation aided the economic factors indicates the importance of

71

political considerations (Nef, 1940). The emergence of capitalism acted upon the guild structure in several ways. A dynamic, expanding economy was inconsistent with the rigid system of guild controls. Some form of distinction between entrepreneur and worker came to replace the distinction between master and journeyman. This distinction arose from the need of the employer for capital rather than technical skill and from the organization of production in the factory system. The role of master was superseded, many of the former masters being reduced to the equivalent of journeymen, and large numbers of these journeymen were thrown together in the factories and correspondingly separated from personal contact with their superiors, which had been possible in a small shop. Efforts to escape from this situation were numerous, yet ultimately unsuccessful. Those weavers who worked in their own cottages found themselves dependent upon suppliers of raw material; as new technology was introduced, they were forced to rent the new equipment, thereby relinquishing ownership over their means of production. Ultimately, the technological advances of the eighteenth century made the factory system dominant in textiles. Competition from marginal members of the labor force, women, children, rural labor, and others, became serious. Even before this the advantages of the division of labor in the reorganization of production had been revealed in the growth of the factory system.

The "labouring poor" (Briefs, 1937) who peopled England in increasing numbers were met by several reactions. The Elizabethan poor laws combined charity with repression. Fear of wandering bands of vagabonds led to the harsh workhouses, perhaps sentiment underlay the locally administered poor rates and wage controls. Laws against the organization of workers came early. The frequency with which these laws were enacted and used suggests that nascent organization was a common occurrence.

The reaction of the workers also lacked consistency. Local strikes, first by journeymen against masters, later by the laboring elements against the owners, were fairly common. Sometimes a local grievance of work conditions was at issue, at other times wages, and at still other times the introduction of machinery was resisted, perhaps by violence. The attack on the inanimate machines perhaps most clearly symbolizes the confused and frightened lashing out of the workers entering the industrial era.

The relationships between the developing middle- and working classes were never quite so clear cut as some theories suggest. The program of the Enlightenment served to unite the energies of both groups during the period of political reform in France. The only indication of a separate program for workers can be found in Babeuf's position, which was of minor significance in the French Revolution. The recognition of a disparity of interests between these groups emerged only gradually; and then it was in part created by members of the bourgeoisie, the self-styled, enlightened leaders of the proletariat.

The workers began to recognize their own interests in part through their closer contact with one another in the factory and in the slum (Renard and Weulersse, 1926, p. 356). An effective basis for mass trade unions was permitted by these conditions. The trade union in part reflected the specific economic demands, which were shared by the workers as a whole, and in part reflected the socialist programs devised by bourgeois intellectuals. Through organization, the workers acquired effective bargaining status, but these organizations have tended to become, in this century, a vested interest rather than a revolutionary force. In western Europe, the socialist programs ultimately assumed political significance in the various Social-Democratic parties. The revolutionary implications of the *Communist Manifesto* were discarded in favor of the extension of the political program of the Enlightenment—the right to vote and parliamentary control.

73

As a consequence, the workers have not tended wholly toward the solidarity of a proletarian class emitting unmitigated hostility toward the bourgeoisie. The recognition of common self-interests among workers led to an effective collaboration, the very effectiveness of which forestalled the socialist prophecies. Society was not crystallized into separate, openly warring classes, rather, conflicts of interest were channelled into existing political institutions. The union and the political party became the expression of class interests; the class itself remained somewhat amorphous.

A psychological identification of workers as a class did develop. But the existence of divisions of interest among the workers, as well as the existence of other cleavages in the larger society, prevented class identification from becoming the sole motivation for group behavior. However, a caste element became apparent in the hereditary nature of this class structure. The permanency and significance of this element is not yet clear.

A caste element of social distance also became noticeable. In part, social distance simply reflected the fact of ecological or physical remoteness between classes. Contact among members of different classes, save in status-defined employment situations (for example, domestic servants), became minimal. Then, too, the heritage of the aristocratic classes of the past was expressed by social distance. The bourgeoisie were all potential parvenus, attempting to achieve higher status through increased wealth and the adoption of new styles of life. Therefore, they could not look with favor upon the universal sharing of privileges but recently won by themselves. Symbols of social distance may have gradually shrunk in significance till only dialect remains (according to the U, Non-U controversy) [Mitford, 1956]. But the rituals of social distance and the maintenance of classes still are characteristic of the West European social order.

What part did the middle class play in the emergence of the working class? Certainly not a fully conscious role. Individual businessmen developed their employment policies and their degree of industrialization in light of the particular conditions of their trade. The fact that their policies all tended to have similar effects stemmed from the similar conditions of profit-making that were available, although conspiracy was also involved (Adam Smith, 1937, pp. 66–67). Undoubtedly numerous entrepreneurs endeavored to force down wages within their own sphere of control. But these actions did not always reflect a conscious class policy. Political repression of the workers was as much a policy of the monarchy as of the bourgeoisie.

The middle-class role was undoubtedly affected by the French Revolution and succeeding periods of violence. As the middle classes achieved the privileges that we have already cited for the city of the Middle Ages, they became hesitant to share these privileges with others. The violence of the "masses" and "mobs" was particularly frightening to those whose privileges were already won. The English reaction to the French Revolution, to Godwin, and to Paine, serves to illustrate this. But the very conservatism and adherence to institutional principle, which Burke came to symbolize, also contained the seeds of the present resolution of the conflict. The emphasis on conciliatory, moderate reform in the middle classes, arising in part from a sentimental moral basis, was able to prevail upon the liking for stability and the dislike of violence of the conservative groups at particular critical junctures. If it appeared to be a choice between outright class war or the extension of privilege, the middle classes chose to yield the privilege.

Thus, the middle classes are responsible, in part, for the development of the working class, but they are also responsible for providing the conciliatory reforms and institutional structure by which open warfare has been avoided. However, even the Code of Napoléon was not sufficient to eliminate the caste elements in the position of the Jews in Western Europe.

American urban social structure developed in a different context from that of western Europe. Nevertheless, the values of the American middle class have roots in the European tradition, and the development of economic institutions had marked parallels in Europe and America, especially in the phase of industrialization. We must identify the distinctive features of the American urban social structure before industrialization and then seek to describe the resulting impact of industrialization upon this structure.

Three factors are commonly held accountable for the existence of a relatively fluid class structure in the United States in the mid-nineteenth century. First, the opposition to a hereditary aristocracy reflected by the Constitution was regarded as a real deterrent to the development of any formally sanctioned elite. Second, the frontier was regarded as a safety valve, an alternative for those who found their class position in the East intolerable. Third, opportunity for social mobility was believed to be widespread.

That these factors were of some significance can scarcely be denied, yet the significance is probably exaggerated. Undue emphasis on them can obscure certain tendencies toward rigidity, especially as they occurred in the older cities of the East and in the plantations of the Hudson Valley and the southern coastal plain. The existence of a middle-class elite, conscious of its class position, is suggested by the various restrictions upon the franchise contained in the state constitutions and also by the plot structure of the contemporary popular novel. Henry Nash Smith has discussed the popular novel and especially the Leather-stocking character in Cooper's novels in this light in *Virgin Land* (Smith, 1957, pp. 64–76). Smith's later chapters especially Chapter XX, "The Garden as Safety Valve," constitute a devastating critique of the frontier as a "safety valve" (pp. 234–45).

Evidence for the opportunity for social mobility usually consists of references to the Horatio Alger stories and to such inspirational addresses as "Acres of Diamonds." Undoubtedly, mobility in America was great in comparison to that of western Europe at the same time. Yet the image of unfettered opportunity that many scholars put forth seems more appropriate to a Chamber of Commerce pamphlet.

Indeed, the American mythology of the nineteenth century fitted too neatly with a Marxist orientation in the twentieth century. One could consistently hold that the preindusrial era was one of great social mobility, but that more recent times bore witness to the hardening of class lines. Such beliefs are themselves important data in the analysis of ideology, and therefore are useful in the interpretation of social class in America, but they have obscured the facts of the matter. Recent research on occupational mobility has found no evidence of hardening of class lines. What, then, is the source of these beliefs?

A main source of egalitarian sentiment can be found in small towns of the Midwest. Contemporary studies, such as *Plainville*, attest to the existence of an egalitarian ideology—"we're all just plain folks" (West, 1945). The sources of this ideology were briefly indicated in Chapter One. Social cleavage in such communities may follow lines of moral respectability, and hard work and church participation are important factors in this cleavage.

This small-town ideology is important not only for its egalitarian effects. From the Civil War to the Great Depression, this ideology was identified with the successful, all-encompassing middle class. Babbitt and Main Street ruled unchallenged (save by Populism). The Roper poll finding that ninety per cent of the American people identified themselves with the middle class can only make sense in terms of the pervasiveness of this ideology (Roper, 1940). Samuel Lubell, in *The Future of American Politics*, examines the political success of the ideology in the post-Depression, post-war era (Lubell, 1956).

The implications of this ideology for social stratification are twofold. First, the ideology sustained a belief in an open society,

77

a society in which hard work and solid morals yielded success, and it successfully resisted inroads of the class ideology or the Socialist ideology (Briefs, 1937, pp. 199–202). Second, special categories of persons were excluded from American culture in this ideology: Negroes, foreigners, and urbanites were accorded unfavorable stereotypes. Groups such as the Know-Nothings and the Ku Klux Klan reflect these views in an extreme form. Just as religion served to unite the medieval commune into a sworn brotherhood of equals, so now religion served to unite the small-town folks and lead them to ideological victory. But outsiders in both instances were excluded. The Oriental Exclusion Acts and the Immigration Laws in part reflect this exclusion, especially the latter.

This small-town ideology in its most distinctive features represents a fusion of the Protestant ethic with frontier elements. The premise that hard work yields or equals success is coupled with egalitarian themes and rituals. The Puritan tradition of New England was carried to the Midwestern town, while the Baptist and Methodist churches became the bulwark of the small town and the small farmer in the South. Further west, the Christian Church developed as a liberal offshoot of the Baptists; it became the third characteristic small-town denomination especially in Oklahoma, Missouri, and Indiana.

Why all this emphasis upon the small town in a study of urban social structure? First, as the political center of gravity moved west, from Jackson on, the small-town ideology became the dominant political ideology. Popular literature and popular culture in general reflected this dominance. Only with Franklin Roosevelt's administration did urban elements finally assume dominance in our national affairs (Lubell, 1956). Failure to reapportion legislative seats at the state level (for instance, Georgia's county units) tends to preserve the small town ideology in the various states and therefore to obscure the extent of the political defeat of the small town. The virtues of the small town

78

are revealed when it is itself in defeat. Riesman's nostalgia for the inner-directed personality can only be felt after urban victory (Riesman, 1950).

Second, the urban middle classes of the period 1850–1900 were made up of the sons and daughters of the small town, turned out in the world to seek their fortune due to the restrictive economy of hometown, yet carriers of the ideology into the nation's commercial and industrial life. Horatio Alger urged them to be true to their ideology, they would then achieve success. On the eastern seaboard, the collapse of patrician oligarchy within the older cities led directly to the victory of the foreign-born, the self-conscious immigrant. But the small-town elements remained the basis of the middle classes, and if they had to conduct a rear guard operation in the politics of the city itself, they still retained much influence from their control of the city's economic life and their strategic location in its social structure. Ultimately, the patricians learned to ally themselves with the immigrant leaders, or more accurately, those who had ascended to the patrician class through economic success did so—Harriman, Rockefeller, Stevenson, Kennedy (who represents a synthesis of both elements), G. Mennen Williams, and Franklin Roosevelt. But the effects of the period when the Chambers of Commerce could with confidence claim to represent America are still with us.

The great population shifts that brought the small town to the fore, and then in turn demolished it, are in part a reflection of the nation's economic life. The agricultural and commercial empire of the mid-nineteenth century was associated with the decentralization of society. But the full-scale development of the Industrial Revolution heralded new trends. The new immigration from southern and eastern Europe, even more than the Irish immigration, revolutionized the composition of the city and led it even farther from the Protestant small town complex. At the same time, the internal migration from rural to urban

79

areas foretold the ultimate shift of political power to the urban areas. In the 1920's the two great prohibitions, of alcohol and of foreigners, constituted the dying gasp of small town political ascendency.

Small-town control obviously coincided with middle-class interests, but the middle class in question included the skilled workers and artisans. The American Federation of Labor under Gompers represented the demands of workers against their employers, but the skilled craftsmen of whom the workers consisted were as thoroughly inbued with the small town ideology as were their employers (Northrup, 1944, pp. 4–14; Briefs, 1937, pp. 196–204). The unskilled laborer, the foreigner, and the Negro were not viewed sympathetically by this élite of the workers (Greer, 1959; Lubell, 1956). If anything, they were viewed as potential competitors on the labor market, to be excluded by regulations like those of the guilds wherever possible (for instance, by apprenticeship restrictions). That the unsuccessful were lazy was the common belief of skilled worker and small business man.

Again, the emergence of the CIO in the Depression indicated a new attitude in labor (Northrup, 1944, pp. 14–16). The organization of industrial unions implied the organization of skilled and unskilled, American and foreign, white and nonwhite, all within the same union local. The economic pressures of the times were sufficiently great to overcome the feelings of social distance among the various ethnic and racial groups.

The exclusion of Orientals and Italians in the Immigration Laws had the somewhat unexpected result that hillbillies, Negroes, Puerto Ricans, and Indians were pulled into the urban labor market in significant volume. The appearance of these groups served to hasten the well-known processes of assimilation for the old ethnic groups. Each new group bears the brunt of hostility and thus relieves the pressures on the previous minority. As second generation fades into third generation, as slum dwelling is replaced by suburban dwelling, as native tongue is

80

replaced by English, as members of one's group achieve economic and political success, each group in turn becomes more at one with traditional America. But this very process changes traditional America.

The assimilation process itself works in unexpected ways. The fact that the political success of the boss depends upon the marginal position of the minority group is well known, but the corollary, that the political success of the boss opens new avenues of success for the minority group members is less well understood. The boss system encouraged the economic success of many minority group members, not merely through graft and patronage, but further, through the protection of various "shady" occupations. The capitalists of the underworld are an integral part of the assimilation process, as William Foote Whyte has stressed in *Street Corner Society* (Whyte, 1955). Here the theme of success through hard work has indeed attained its most bizarre expression.

As the assimilation process continues, the corrosive effects on small-town ideology grow with it. In particular, the stereotypes for the various foreign groups lose their clarity and their force—certain jokes no longer seem humorous to a new generation. But where does the process end? Does each group automatically ride up the social structure, as on an escalator, or are some groups condemned to the position of a pariah in our society? To deal with these questions requires a closer analysis of social structure than has been previously attempted in this study.

First, let us review the main question of this chapter, and the extent to which we have answered it. We wish to comprehend the social structure of contemporary urban America. We have witnessed the emergence of a novel system of social equality in Western Europe, which has itself been succeeded by new divisions within society, in part due to the emergence of an industrial economy. Symbolic expressions of social inequality have become less pronounced, but the remnants of the aristocracy provided models of snobbery to which the parvenue could aspire, thus encouraging the presence of fine gradations in dress, dialect, and way of life by which each rather stable social group could be identified. The position of the Jew also remained marginal in this society, as we have been so harshly reminded in this century.

We have tried to depict the essential features of American social structure prior to industrialization, the manner in which industrialization itself brought new racial and ethnic groups onto the urban scene, and the process of assimilation of these groups into the existing social structure. The picture is something like this. A dominant class system in the East was gradually losing political and ideological significance because of the rise to power of a relatively classless Middle West. But the broad middle class emerging in the Middle West had its own limits of inclusiveness as well. Catholics, Jews, foreigners, and Negroes tended to be excluded as participants in this system (Warner and Srole, 1945, pp. 283–296). The nature and extent of exclusion varies in each case, but the fact of this exclusion underlies the main characteristics of current social structure. These groups were also consistently ranked low within the existing urban class-system.

The main cleavage in modern America has not been along class lines but along racial and ethnic lines. This has been true to such an extent that the racial and ethnic cleavages have obscured, and so prevented, the emergence of an economic class-system. The small-town Protestant ideology of the Middle West supported the ethnic cleavages but denied the class cleavages, thus supplying the beliefs appropriate to the existing social structure (Myrdal, 1944, p. 713).

The middle classes have never despised workers as such— given their ideological emphasis upon hard work they could not. But they have despised the immigrant, the irresponsible, the unclean. Trade unions and socialism could be condemned as foreign ideologies in the manner in which the "anarchists" were condemned in the Haymarket Riots (Browne, 1924, pp. 74–105). But as pointed out above, the dominant force in the union movement, the American Federation of Labor, reflected much the same views, thereby preventing the formation of any sentiments of solidarity among workers as a class.

Much weight has been given to the "closing of the frontier" as a factor in the development of social classes in America. The hypothesis is that the safety valve of opportunity was lost. But the view sketched above gives very little support to this hypothesis. Large-scale industrialization and urbanization would have had the same effects if the frontier had remained open. It was the myth of opportunity that was crucial to the small-town egalitarian ideology, not the universal fact of opportunity. Rogoff's finding that the rates of social mobility in Indianapolis have not changed in this century is entirely consistent with this analysis (Rogoff, 1953). The amount of opportunity probably has not changed, but the belief in it has. Lubell is right in drawing our attention to the "urban frontier," the slum out of which the immigrants fought their way to opportunity, as the continuation of Indian Territory in our national life (Lubell, 1956). Primeval forest has been succeeded by asphalt jungle.

However, the processes affecting social structure today may not be readily inferred from this analysis of the past. Tolerance of various minority groups has been forced upon us as members of these groups have acceded to power. No politician dependent upon urban votes can afford to offend these groups; in particular, the form of the electoral college makes the presidency especially subject to these pressures—much more so than the legislature. Since the Supreme Court is selected by the president, it is no surprise that the Court and the legislature should be at odds. The extent of this tolerance is so great that movie actresses no longer need change their names from Novak to Jones in order to please mass audiences. Lucille Ball and Desi Arnaz can portray an ideal happy family in this new cultural climate. Heroes in popular fiction may soon follow suit, if indeed, they have not already done so.

The tolerance of minority groups has been, in other contexts, explained by an alleged vanquishment of caste by class on the urban scene. The general activity and change in urban society, large numbers of interactions among persons, and instability of the social order are felt to be inconsistent with the rituals and the rigidity of caste structure, and therefore with all elements of caste. But the ethnic segregation of the Jews and other "pariah peoples" does not support such optimism. In particular, if specific ethnic minorities are forced into undesirable occupations, then the rituals of social distance would certainly resemble rituals of caste distinction, though, of course, they (the rituals) would not necessarily become rationalized by a common religious system. Perhaps some caste elements will not flourish in the city, but class will not, therefore, become the only element in social structure.

Indeed, if we turn our attention to the scapegoat phenomenon, and relate it to the existence of spatially segregated minorities in cities, then we may be led to an opposite conclusion. Namely, that social distance preserves the existence of ethnically or racially defined scapegoats as outlets for the "frustrations of the masses" or means for those who wish to manipulate the population. Certainly Hitler's reiteration of *"Blut und Boden"* (Blood and Soil) is not explicable in terms of social class or economic class. If we recall that Maine paralleled the legal changes from status to contract with loyalty changes from kinship to area, and if we then turn our attention to the phenomenon of nationalism is the recent history of the world, perhaps we can envision alternatives to social class as a basis for antagonism and conflict (Maine, 1885, pp. 125–128).

Weber remarked that, "every technological repercussion and

84

economic transformation threatens stratification by status and pushes the class situation into the foreground" (Weber, 1946, pp. 193–194). He failed to relate these repercussions to ethnic segregation and the scapegoat phenomenon. Yet he correctly predicted the emergence of a strong, self-conscious union movement in the American depression with this proposition. And the lack of socialistic emphasis or class conflict in the union movement during the long postwar prosperity seems also in accord with his views. But will a new depression necessarily solidify conflict around class lines, or will the frustrations generated be displaced against particular ethnic groups? How will the political situation affect either possibility?

Clearly, two minorities have always been the leading candidates for scapegoats in America, the Negroes and the Jews. What factors could mitigate against their selection in the future? Currently, the large number of other minorities engaged in assimilating themselves have something common to gain by tolerance for all. But similarly, they feel the pressures of discrimination from above and may choose to pass it along to the less successful minorities. In other words, a coalition of minorities for tolerance is not assured.

The point is this. Considerations of urban social psychology lead us to be cautious in predictions that class will become the sole element in American urban social structure in any foreseeable future. To the extent that class dominates, it will be in part a reflection of changing economic conditions, especially fluctuations of the business cycle. Ethnic segregation may still be with us and may greatly affect the nature and functions of a social class system.

5

Social Structure and
Residential Areas

NOW we turn our attention to some recent research upon a
number of American cities. The interpretive background of the
previous chapter will aid us in unraveling the theoretical issues
involved in this research. In the present chapter we shall confine
our attention to research on the social characteristics of areas
of cities. Most of this research employs mapping techniques to
reveal the spatial distribution of social characteristics. The
United States Bureau of the Census publications of census tract

data provide these researchers with their basic statistics (Census, 1952).

Our problem is to describe the spatial distribution of the social characteristics of cities. The regularities of the spatial distribution provide clues to the aggregate social structure of the city. Of course, there is much more to urban social structure than can be revealed on maps, especially maps of census data only. But if there is any aggregate, over-all urban social structure, its effects should be revealed in spatial regularities.

Our initial definition of social structure requires that behavioral consequences must be revealed for social structure to exist. And in our earlier discussion we have established that residential location should reveal the effects of social structure. The "style of life" of a person, the income of a person, and the prejudices of a person are all reflected in his choice of dwelling. Surely, social class and ethnic theories contain predictions that can be tested on these data.

Further, there is no alternative set of data by which we can readily depict the aggregate social structure of the city. Only by mapping our data can we readily grasp this totality. If the city is defined as both a spatial and a social entity, in the manner of Parsons and Hawley, then mapping is a required method of study (Parsons, 1951; Hawley, 1950).

What sorts of regularities can be revealed on a map? How can these regularities be explained by theories of urban social structure? These questions will guide us throughout the chapter.

First, suppose we have only one characteristic to consider. Then, the regularities possible can all be described as clusters. Either the spatial distribution of the characteristic is random, in which case no clustering or pattern will be revealed, or the spatial distribution is not random, and we can then describe the resulting configuration. The regularities appear as geometrical configurations on the map—a two-dimensional space if we use distinctive color schemes to stand for presence or absence of the characteristic or varying degrees of the characteristics. But if we erect a line segment in the center of each small area of the city, and then draw connecting lines between the tops of the lines of contiguous or adjacent areas, we shall construct a surface in three dimensions. Visually, the surface will resemble a patchwork of clothes lines, or telephone poles. But if the planes between these connecting lines are filled in, the surface will resemble a mountain range or some other geographical phenomenon. It will be useful to employ geographical or topographical terminology in describing the configurations that may result.

The surface we have constructed will actually consist of many facets. But if we increase the number of small areas in the city, or decrease the size of the small areas, then we increase the number of vertical lines, and therefore tend to "smooth out" the surface—generate curves rather than straight lines.

While a number of complex patterns are conceivable for such a surface, we shall be interested in a fairly simple class of surfaces. It is possible to imagine surfaces that look like a group of volcanoes, or a group of Pike's Peaks, or a series of parallel mountain ranges interspersed with canyons. But such surfaces are not especially likely for social characteristics. At least, if they were common we would have to abandon our usual notions of social structure. We may expect that similar social characteristics are more likely to occur in adjacent areas, thereby giving the impression of a plateau or a gently rising slope. Occasional steep slopes may occur, marking perhaps the contrast between neighborhoods on the opposite sides of a railroad track. But for the most part we would expect either level areas or a fairly constant slope in such a surface.

We could proceed to map each characteristic this way in turn and examine the resulting surface. But we might also be curious to see how similar the surfaces are for several characteristics. In general, we might be interested in the relationships among such surfaces. One procedure to achieve this purpose would involve grouping together those characteristics having quite similar surfaces, and then contrasting the different types of surfaces among groups of characteristics. We shall follow a procedure of this sort as far as previous research will permit us.

Another way of stating our problem is this. First, we must choose relevant social characteristics. Second, we must map these characteristics. Third, we must analyze and interpret the resulting surfaces for these characteristics.

Since we are dependent upon the census tract publications for our initial data, several limitations are placed on our resulting research. We can only study the distributions of those characteristics that the census chose to gather information on and tabulate; we must rely upon the census definitions for the characteristics; and we are also dependent upon the small areas —census tracts—the census used for computing the basic statistics we are employing.

Research upon the relevant social characteristics has been performed by Shevky and Bell, with subsequent studies by Tryon, Schmid, and the author (Shevky and Bell, 1955; Bell, 1955; Tryon, 1955; Van Arsdol, Camillert, and Schmid, 1958; Beshers, 1957). Shevky and Bell have examined census data from San Francisco in 1940 and 1950 and have derived three "social area indices," which they regard as completely describing urban social structure. Investigations of other cities by Tryon, Schmid, and the author have confirmed the general empirical findings of Shevky and Bell. But the theoretical issues involved in interpreting these findings have not been resolved in this research. We shall review the empirical findings of this line of research first, then turn our attention to the theoretical issues. Note that this research is based upon characteristics of areas, which are not equivalent to characteristics of individuals. We can clarify some of the theoretical issues by comparing findings based on the characteristics of individuals with findings based on the characteristics of areas.

The findings of Shevky and Bell are based on the analysis of census tract data. A number of variables can be taken directly from the census tract manual or can be constructed from the data reported in this manual. When the relationships between these variables are examined it is found that the variables may be separated into three groups. Within these groups the variables are fairly closely related, while the relationships among variables in different groups are small by comparison. This result is so clear that practically any statistical procedure will reveal it (Beshers, 1960, pp. 52–73).

The largest group of closely related variables seem to be related to *socioeconomic status*. Such variables as income, education, occupation, rental, housing value, and per cent employed all tend to cluster together. This result would be expected on the basis of a large number of surveys of individuals in the social-stratification research literature. Nevertheless, it is of some interest to see that the results hold for the characteristics of small areas—the census tracts—as well. Shevky and Bell regard this group of variables as indexes of social rank.

The second group of variables, called *segregation or ethnic status*, sometimes consists of the single variable per cent Negro, and sometimes includes per cent of other races and of foreign-born white from southern and eastern Europe (Shevky and Bell, 1955, pp. 17–18). These variables seem related to the various social-distance findings that have been reported from surveys of individuals. Presumably all of these minorities are segregated in roughly the same pattern in all of these cities, though the data do not establish this point completely. In particular, we need data from earlier censuses in order to determine the effect of assimilation upon ethnic segregation.

The third group of variables, called *urbanization or family status*, includes fertility, per cent of women at work, and per cent of single-family dwelling units. These variables do not represent a familiar finding for research on individuals. Nor

91

are they, save for the architectural clue in the third variable, especially characteristic of previous research on areas. Possibly the contrast between apartment-house modes of life and separate-home modes of life accounts for such differences between areas.

Interpretation of the first two groups of variables is vastly simpler than interpretation of the third. Let us consider the first group. Our previous discussion have given great attention to the formation of economic cleavages within an industrial society. But economic differentials are, obviously, associated with occupational and educational differentials. Indeed, if the small-town emphasis upon work as a factor in success contains within it the concept of work as an end in itself, occupation should be an important element in our social structure. Not simply the acquisition of material goods, but the nature of the work itself should be among the factors distinguishing social strata. Research employing survey procedures confirms this view—that is, that occupation is a more satisfactory index of prestige ranking in American communities than income (Kahl, 1957).

Note that this interpretation of prestige ranking is consistent with Weber's view quoted earlier. That is, that prestige factors, or stratification by status, tend to operate during "normal" times while economic cleavages become significant during periods of economic stress or technological change. Thus, if prestige is largely determined by occupation in American society, then occupation would be the best index of prestige ranking during "normal" times.

Thus, the first group of variables suggest to us that indexes of social stratification with which we are familiar, both in theory and in survey research, turn out to be closely associated with areas. The fact is not especially surprising, but it does require further clarification and explanation. In particular, we would like to determine why in this instance "birds of a feather flock together." Does it simply represent different patterns of expenditure on consumer's goods?—more simple, different capacities to purchase consumer's goods? Does it reflect some underlying regularities of land values? And if so, what determines the land values?

For the second group of variables, racial and ethnic, much the same conclusion can be reached. They are familiar to us in theory and in research on individuals. The fact that they are associated with areas suggests segregation resulting from social distance. This type of explanation will be pursued with the help of studies of spatial distribution.

→ The third group of variables, family characteristics, must be handled differently. There is no clear theoretical basis for regarding these variables as aspects of urban social structure. Shevky and Bell disagree between themselves (1955, p. 68). Nor has there been any previous research that might serve as a guide in such an analysis. Some further data bearing on this group of variables will be examined, but not as elements of social structure.

The results of the Shevky-Bell research simplify our further work with census tract data. We can assume that the closely related variables will have rather similar patterns of spatial distribution. Thus, instead of thirty or more variables we have three groups of variables to study by mapping procedures. Shevky and Bell have suggested indexes for each of these groups of variables (1955, pp. 54–58). These indexes are composites of the variables in each group. Some use of these indexes has been made in the study of spatial distributions.

However, most of the important empirical and theoretical work on spatial distribution of social characteristics has not employed the Shevky-Bell indexes. We may relate the two types of research if we note that rent, occupation, and per cent nonwhite are the census variables most often used in these studies. Either rent or occupation may be used as rough indexes of the variables in the socioeconomic status group. Rent in particular is often used because it can be computed for a series of censuses, thereby permitting historical trend analysis. Most of the other census variables have been changed or redefined so drastically that historical comparisons are not very useful. Even with rent there are some technical problems, which we need not go into here (Beshers, 1957, pp. 49–50). Per cent nonwhite may be used alone to stand for ethnic status, thus also permitting historical analysis. Family status may be represented by fertility or simply by the per cent of children under five in the population of the census tract.

We may now proceed to the literature on the spatial distribution of these social characteristics. First, we should review the classical schemes of Burgess and of Hoyt (Burgess, 1925; Hoyt, 1939). Burgess's name has become associated with the geometric pattern of concentric circles of social characteristics surrounding the central business district. If we try to visualize Burgess's pattern in terms of the topographical scheme described above, we may think of the socioeconomic status variables as taking on low values near the central business district and then increasing as the distance from the central business district increases. The pattern will resemble an amphitheatre or football stadium in which the circular rows of seats stand for consecutive concentric zones. A similar descriptive notion is that of the gradient of social characteristics, also suggested by Burgess, which amounts to a smoother rise from center outwards, that is, a structure like a salad bowl. Empirical research by Calvin Schmid, among others, tended to confirm this general notion (Schmid, 1944).

Burgess's explanations for this distribution of social characteristics are of two sorts. First, the undesirable zone in transition next to the central business district is created and maintained by economic processes. If we assume the continued expansion of the central business district out into the surrounding older residential areas, these latter areas are potentially of high land value when converted to commercial use. But there will be an intervening period in which land-use patterns designed to return the greatest immediate profit with the least expenditures of capital improvements will be prevalent in these areas. Subdivided rooming houses, flop houses, shabby and shady businesses will be typical. Second, Burgess assumes that the more desirable residential areas will be found at increasing distances from the zone in transition, with the most desirable areas far out in the suburbs. An explanation in terms of land values is possible, for it may be argued that land values tend to be similar in contiguous areas, therefore the least similar land values would be the farthest apart.

But it may be asked whether the explanation in terms of land values is entirely satisfactory. For the land values reflect the desirability of the land to the purchaser. While desirability of commercial property, or of industrial property, may be largely determined by economic considerations, the desirability of residential areas would seem to be a more complex phenomenon; quite general cultural factors would seem to effect residential desirability. In particular, the general evaluations of types of people may be carried over to the areas in which they live. Further, characteristics of American residential areas such as separate homes, immaculate green lawns, and so on, seem to reflect American cultural values rather than to reflect inexorable economic laws.

This type of criticism of Burgess was expressed by Walter Firey in *Land Use in Central Boston* (Firey, 1946). Cultural factors are shown to influence the pattern of land use in Boston, especially the preservation of the Boston Common. Firey argues that the Common is a symbol of historic sentiments, and that allegiance to these sentiments by the citizens of Boston prevents the land from being converted to commercial use.

Form also has suggested that land uses and land values are manipulated by various human agencies (Form, 1954). For example, real-estate agents have much to gain by such activities.

95

Actions of city-planning commissions and zoning commissions may affect land values, and Form suggests that study of the ways in which these organizations operate would throw light on the distribution of land values in cities.

Hoyt examined the spatial distribution of rent in 142 American cities in the 1930's using block data. His observations confirm the notion that there is a high-rent area from which the rental values gradually decline until the lowest rental areas are reached (Hoyt, 1939, p. 74). Typically, this high-rent area is found on the edge of a city; but it does not constitute a concentric circle, rather a sector beginning at the center of the city and widening as it approaches the periphery. The sectors are either homogeneous in rental values or constantly rising in values and may be partly defined by radial transportation lines. Although Hoyt comments upon factors that may account for this distribution, he does not provide a fully elaborated explanation.

Given these general descriptions of the distribution of the socioeconomic factor, we may ask what evidence is available for interpreting this distribution in terms of social structure. A study of occupational distributions in Chicago by Duncan and Duncan is relevant (Duncan and Duncan, 1955). The study reveals that, "spatial distances between occupation groups are closely related to their social distances, measured either in terms of conventional indicators of socio-economic status or in terms of differences in occupational origins; that the most segregated occupation groups are those at the extremes of the socio-economic scale; that concentration of residence in low-rent areas is inversely related to socio-economic status; and that centralization of residence is likewise inversely related to socio-economic status" (p. 295; Beshers, 1957, pp. 34–44). (Centralization refers to proximity to central business district.)

More detailed information by Duncan and Duncan is even more helpful. The census category "clerical and kindred workers" may be contrasted with the census category "craftsmen, foremen, and kindred workers." The clerical workers have edu-

96

cational backgrounds similar to the higher white-collar occupations, are generally believed to share in the high prestige of the white-collar occupations, presumably have similar values to those of the other white-collar occupations, but they have far less income than the craftsmen and foremen. Therefore, if financial means are the most important factor in the distribution of the occupational groups, the craftsmen and foremen would live in or near the neighborhoods of sales workers, managers, and professionals. But if the clerical workers live more closely to these high-prestige neighborhoods, then desire for prestige must be more important to them than to the craftsmen and foremen. The Duncan's analysis "clearly places the clerical group closer to the other white-collar groups than the craftsmen-foremen are, and the clerical workers' index of low-rent concentration is less than that of the craftsmen and foremen. But in terms of residential centralization the clerical group tends to fall with the lower blue-collar groups, and the craftsmen-foremen group with the other white-collar groups. In general, it would appear that 'social status' or prestige is more important in determining the residential association of clerical with other white-collar groups than is income, although the latter sets up a powerful cross-pressure, as evidenced by the comparatively high rent-income ratio of clerical families" (1955, pp. 502–503).

Thus preference for similar prestige in neighbors must accompany strictly economic considerations in residential location of occupational groups. But we do not know whether any negative factors are involved for occupational groups as they are involved for ethnic or racial groups. Probably a direct study of attitudes would be necessary to decide this question.

The fact of discrimination against and segregation of various minorities has been observed many times. Roughly, the generalizations use the cohesiveness of a common culture and the discrimination by the existing population to explain the existence of these segregated areas and employ the notion of assimilation to describe the processes by which segregation is broken down.

Wirth's study, *The Ghetto*, traces out some of these processes for the Jews of Chicago, emphasizing especially the dynamics by which the established and more assimilated member of the minority group is himself repelled by the new arrivals and flees to a new area, only to find that the others have fled with him (Wirth, 1928). Friction between the established German Jews and the newly arriving Russian Jews was not uncommon. Similar friction in Boston between immigrants from North Italy and the subsequent Sicilian immigrants is noted by William Foote Whyte in *Street Corner Society* (Whyte, 1944). Jerome K. Myers has studied the processes by which assimilated Italians move to high-prestige areas of New Haven (Myers, 1950) and points out that the desire to "get ahead" stimulates such movement as well as the desire to avoid the newcomers.

The documentation of these processes with Chicago census data is provided by Duncan and Lieberson (Duncan and Lieberson, 1959). They divide the immigrant groups into "old" immigrants and "new" immigrants by country of origin. Thus, the foreign-born white from England and Wales, Sweden, Germany, and Ireland are included among "old" immigrants, while the other European countries provide "new" immigrants. They find that both old and new immigrant groups were segregated from native whites in 1930 and 1950. The old immigrants were less segregated but also less changed during the time period. However, the second generation of the old immigrants moved away faster than the second generation of the new immigrants. In both 1930 and 1950, the rank of the nationality groups in degree of segregation was the same.

Furthermore, the foreign-born white were segregated from each other. Though this pattern of segregation is somewhat similar to the pattern of segregation from native whites there are a number of differences. The authors reject the notion of a foreign "ghetto" on the basis of this data. They feel that a picture of separate "colonies" is more accurate. These colonies are fairly stable. However, they tend to be found near the downtown area. Both old and new immigrants moved out (decentralized) from 1930 to 1950, but the old immigrants were further out at both times.

In order to relate their research to the findings of interviews, Duncan and Lieberson show that various measures of assimilation (such as literacy) and various measures of socioeconomic status (such as occupation) correlate with their pattern of segregation. Furthermore, this pattern of segregation is similar to the ranking of nationality groups as determined by Bogardus's social-distance scale.

But the situation for Jews and Negroes is not exactly parallel to that of the nationality groups. Census data on Jews is not available in the United States since there have been no questions on religion recently. However, Duncan has examined the census data for Montreal, Canada, and has found the Jews to be considerably more segregated than any of the other religious groups (Duncan, 1959). Similarly, the Jews were considerably more segregated than any ethnic groups. The Duncan and Lieberson research on Chicago showed that "Negroes are much more segregated than any immigrant group (Duncan and Lieberson, 1959. p. 373). Thus we cannot conclude that the experience of assimilation can be carried over to these two minorities.

The patterns of Negro segregation in Chicago have long been systematically investigated by sociologists. Hoyt verified the existence of similar patterns of segregation and noted some patterns of the intensity of segregation as a consequence of size of the white and Negro populations of cities (Hoyt, 1939, pp. 62–71). The most detailed study employing census data is *The Negro Population of Chicago* by Duncan and Duncan (Duncan and Duncan, 1957).

The fact of active discrimination against Negroes can be inferred from the census data. In the pattern of expansion of the

99

Negro areas, no area that has become predominantly Negro has subsequently reverted to other racial use (although this finding seems somewhat specific to Chicago, witness Georgetown in Washington, D.C.). Indeed, "a decrease seldom occurred, once an area had reached a proportion of say, 10 percent Negroes" (Duncan and Duncan, 1957, p. 11). Social distance is clearly reflected in this finding. But the fact that Negroes have to pay higher rents than whites must pay for comparable housing certainly reflects discrimination against the Negro in the housing market. For, if all housing were equally available to Negroes other than in price alone, one would expect them to avail themselves of the cheaper rental properties, especially since Negro incomes are, on the average, substantially lower than white incomes. A lack of housing alternatives also helps to account for the increase of crowding, which continues in those areas that have become at least 99 per cent Negro, the "piling-up" tracts. One final bit of evidence can be gleaned from home-ownership data. Although the Negro population "invading" a white area has population characteristics similar to those of the whites in the area, the Negroes become greater purchasers of homes than their predecessors. The Duncans interpret this finding as a consequence of an effort to escape from the exorbitant rents (Duncan and Duncan, 1957, p. 16).

Within the Negro population, processes take place that are similar to the movement of the assimilated Jews or assimilated Italians described above. Not only are the old-timers typically involved in invading new white territory but the completely Negro areas seem to serve as ports of entry for migrants from outside the city. The continued increases in density may be associated with particular patterns of doubling up in migration. For example, one's loyalty to one's kin may require sharing living space if no alternative is available, but the census data cannot reveal such information. Generally, the expansion of the Negro areas is outward from the center of the city. Thus a zonal pattern of the sort suggested by Burgess is revealed, with the most desirable residential areas farthest from the center of the city. Further evidence for the operation of social distance among the Negroes themselves is contained in the distribution of occupations within the Negro areas. Occupations are segregated to the same degree and in the same pattern as the Duncans found for the city of Chicago as a whole. Minor exceptions seemed to result from the differing characteristics of the "salesmen" category between Negroes and whites. Thus the "assimilated" Negro tends to escape from the least desirable areas, yet he is unable to escape from Negro areas themselves. For, wherever he goes, he tends to bring the Negro areas with him. The plight of the Negro middle classes, seeking to rise further in social status yet followed close behind by less successful Negroes, is clearly reflected in these data.

So far the census data have served as most useful reflections of theories of social structure. When we turn to the spatial distribution of per cent of children, the picture is far less clear. First, the distribution of children is not related to either of the first two variables. Yet it is a fact that, for the city of Cleveland, children are segregated to roughly the same extent as non-whites and as rental values (Beshers, 1957, pp. 74–98). Further, the per cent of children increases in a gradient pattern as one moves outward from the center of Cleveland. These findings appear to be contradictory; at the very least they are confusing.

The most sensible resolution of these findings runs something like this. The distribution of children is related to the distribution of dwelling units with multiple rooms. Such dwelling units are more commonly separate dwelling units than they are apartments, thus accounting for the decentralization of children. But the rental values of these multiple-room dwelling units varies extensively, so that families, in seeking more room, need not necessarily seek higher rents. This suggestion is in line with Rossi's finding that families move in response to increasing num-

101

bers of children (Rossi, 1955). In other words, the distribution of children over the city is a consequence of the distribution of architectural or physical phenomena more than it is a consequence of any familiar social variables.

What sorts of conclusions can we come to with respect to these data? First of all, the picture of smoothly changing surfaces seems reasonably valid when one observes the city as a whole. Similar characteristics seem to be clustered closely together. Roughly, the more similar the characteristics, the closer they are found together, and conversely, the less similar the characteristics, the farther they are found apart. Studies of rental values, occupations, and racial groups attest to this principle.

But are all the clusterings of characteristics to be explained by the same principles? Certainly, the correspondence between prestige of occupations as measured by interviews and the distribution of occupational groups spatially suggests prestige attraction as one broad principle. Another related principle, that of social distance, is suggested by the correspondence between interview findings and the distribution of racial and ethnic groups. In fact, these two principles seem to be special cases of a more general principle—which might be named social desirability. Prestige attraction is the positive expression of this principle and social distance is the negative expression of it.

But this general principle obviously takes different forms in special cases. As pointed out at the beginning of this chapter, there are at least three mechanisms that, operating separately or together, could result in these kinds of clustering. First, the differential distribution of income; second, the preference for similar neighbors; and third, the rejection of dissimilar neighbors.

If income were the sole determinant of residential location, then the ecological discussion of land values would seem to be the relevant approach to explaining the clustering effect. But the research of the Duncans indicates that income does not operate

102

alone. We may suggest that the other two principles operate to define land values (although, of course, still other principles also help to define land values, such as proximity to work, distance from obnoxious industrial areas, natural beauty of site, and so on). In fact, we found that clerical workers were willing to spend excess amounts of money to obtain a prestige location, whereas Negroes were forced to spend excess amounts of money in order to obtain any location. Clearly, these latter two principles operate in different ways. The difference results from the fact that one is the positive expression of social desirability and the other is the negative expression.

If one belongs to racial or ethnic groups that are generally discriminated against, then both the positive and the negative effects of social desirability will determine one's residential location. Thus, the Negro population of Chicago is segregated from the white population; yet the high-prestige Negro occupations are segregated from the low-prestige Negro occupations. However, if one belongs to racial or ethnic groups that are not generally discriminated against, only the positive expression of social desirability will apply.

A further consequence of the negative expression has implications for the degree of clustering of these characteristics. One may suppose that the degree of clustering when both positive and negative effects are operating would be greater than the clustering for positive alone. One may further suggest that the negative effect would be greater than the positive effect. The positive effect operates through the individual's preferences as to income expenditure, and is subject to much individual variation, but the negative effect operates through the formal and informal norms of discrimination and is applied equally to all discernible members of the minority group.

To date, the appropriate research on degree of clustering has not been undertaken. If we consider the spatial clustering between census tract averages, over the entire city then all three of our Shevky-Bell indexes are clustered about equally. But if we consider clustering within the census tracts and within blocks, then the results may be different. Leslie Kish has begun to investigate this type of within-tract and within-block clustering (Kish, 1959). His preliminary results indicate that within-block clustering is extremely high for nonwhites, moderate in correlation with varying income groups, and negligible for most other social characteristics. Thus, his preliminary results are consistent with the speculation in the two paragraphs above.

One further theoretical problem remains. As noted in earlier chapters, the creation of a Negro ghetto in Chicago is hardly consistent with the belief that class automatically replaces caste in an urban-industrial society. What sorts of explanations can be invoked for this phenomenon? While theories of frustration, aggression, social unrest, and prejudice account in part for the phenomenon, other theories may supplement the explanation.

Our problem may be restated in another way. If we compare the discrimination of whites toward Negroes in the South with the discrimination of whites toward Negroes in the urban North (there are very few Negroes in the rural North), we see that the patterns of behavior are somewhat different. The ultimate question that the southerner will pose in a defense of segregation is, "Would you have your daughter marry a Negro?" In contrast, the northerner seems infinitely more concerned for his real-estate investments. At least, the northerner will ask, "Would you have a Negro live next door to you?" and defend his concern for this question by quoting various statements about a resulting fall in real-estate values. Interracial violence in the South is often justified as protecting white women, while violence in the North is often aimed at protecting white neighborhoods. Obviously, many northerners are concerned about their daughters and many southerners are concerned about their dollars. But these different responses provide clues for speculation, if not convincing empirical evidence.

The southerner's concern for his daughter is often interpreted in Freudian, if not outright sexual terms. Dollard stresses the sexual advantage for white males in the segregated situation, with a monopoly on white females plus access to nonwhite females (Dollard, 1937). An alternative interpretation relies upon Maine's observation of an evolution from kinship to local contiguity as a basis for personal loyalties (Maine, 1885). We may consider this an evolution resulting in a changed basis for prestige. The southerner's concern for whom his daughter marries may be a reflection of a kinship-dominated society in which alliances by marriage supply the most significant prestige. The northerner's concern for his neighbors may reflect the importance of neighborhood in determining prestige.

The anthropologists' observations that kinship is the essential element in social structure is relevant here (Radcliffe-Brown, 1952). In the relatively stable, nonindustrial society, kinship is indeed crucial for determining social structure. If the society practices a settled form of agriculture, the significant form of wealth is likely to be land. But often land will not be transferrable by ordinary transactions within the legal system of the society. The only way to get ahead in this society is to marry wisely. Since the selection of daughter's husband determines the entire fate of the family fortune, it becomes a matter for the parents to decide. Those not familiar with anthropological literature may reflect upon the situation in medieval Europe. The relationship between land ownership, prestige, the nobility as a distinct social group, and the meaning of marital alliances may become clear.

Exactly why neighborhood should become the important issue when the importance of kinship declines is by no means clear. Certainly, few urban northerners have much to do with their neighbors, and certainly, the home is the largest single investment of many middle-class families, but this seems not to be a convincing explanation in itself.

We may speculate that contact with the neighbors is in fact pertinent to this issue. Who daughter marries has something to do with who daughter meets. Daughter will not come into contact with Negroes in an integrated school because residential segregation of nonwhites effectively yields segregation of school districts. Residence choice and marriage choice may be closely connected.

Now let us consider two puzzling empirical problems—one pertaining to Georgetown in Washington, D.C., and the other pertaining to Charleston, South Carolina. Georgetown is an area originally inhabited by wealthy upper-class whites in large homes (Editors of Fortune, 1958, pp. 25, 109). Impoverished Negroes moved into this area and were housed in squalid crowded conditions in these homes but years later, wealthy whites returned and began to displace the Negro inhabitants. During the process of displacement, wealthy whites and impoverished Negroes lived side by side. How could this be?

First, the return of whites to Georgetown was in part related to the kind of historical sentiments toward old houses that Firey describes as occurring in Boston, particularly with respect to beleaguered Beacon Hill. But does not the contact with their neighbors disturb the whites? We may speculate that the social worlds of these two groups are so disparate that contact of a sort that might be construed as egalitarian never takes place between them. Contact thus does not reflect social equality, and, therefore, has none of the implications that we might expect from contacts as equals. In particular, the whites send their children to private schools, country clubs, yacht clubs, and so forth, so that informal contact at a tender age is unlikely.

Charleston was not the capital of the Confederacy, but from many points of view it was the epitome of the Confederacy. Yet Hoyt's data reveal less segregation of nonwhites in Charleston than in most other American cities (Hoyt, 1939, pp. 66–67).

Closer inspection reveals that whites and nonwhites are commonly found within the same blocks, but that the whites live in the large houses on the main streets and that the Negroes live in former slave quarters, which line the alleys between the main streets. Clearly, contact between these two groups will reflect inequalities stemming from the historical conditions of slavery.

The southern position is often summarized by the saying, "So long as they stay in their place I don't care what they do." The contact implications of residential proximity depend upon the cultural definitions of such social relationships. For the southerner, close contacts with Negroes are fine, so long as the Negroes are deferent. The northerner does not recognize this distinction.

The over-all view taken in this chapter may be summarized as follows. Shevky, Bell, and Tryon are primarily interested in studying the social characteristics of areas, but they are less interested in the spatial distribution of these characteristics. For them, social structure is defined solely in terms of the relations among characteristics. Park, Burgess, Hoyt, and Duncan are interested in studying the spatial distribution of social characteristics. They cite relationships between patterns of spatial distribution and research using interview methods. But the path taken in this volume has been to state a theory of urban social structure, deduce from this theory the consequences for patterns of social characteristics of areas, and then test the deductions with area data.

The empirical data dealt with here largely confirm classical notions of urban social structure. But in doing so they permit simplification of our aggregate theories of urban social structure. In particular they permit us to relate occupational segregation, ethnic segregation, and racial segregation as variations within the general processes of stratification of society. The difference among these variations are great, yet similarities exist as well.

To many readers this chapter may have merely confirmed the obvious. Yet the obvious as well as the obscure must be explained by our theories. If our theories do not explain the obvious, we may discard them lightheartedly. The theory of urban social structure passes this test.

6

Consequences of Spatial Distribution

IN the previous chapter, we saw that various social characteristics are distributed over the city in a definite pattern. This pattern seems to be predictable from stratification theories. In this chapter and the next, we shall take this patterned distribution as given. We shall seek to elucidate its consequences.

These consequences are of two general types. If we recall the discussion of ecology and functionalism in Chapter Two, the distinction between manifest and latent causal relationships can be brought to mind. Specifically, we must distinguish between those causal relationships that must be recognized or believed in (in the sense of the Thomas's theorem) before they can exist and those causal relationships that do not depend upon the recognition or awareness of the individual. The former relationship leads us into the realm of social psychology, the latter leads us into ecology (as defined in this book).

In the present chapter we shall restrict our attention to the ecological types of consequences. These are all of the same general type—given a particular spatial distribution of persons, what consequences follow for their social behavior? Space, in such statements, is regarded as an environmental limitation upon behavior.

Statements of this sort lead into one general kind of difficulty. They tend to imply a determinism of a sort generally agreed to be objectionable in the social sciences. Sociologists who follow Weber insist upon a voluntaristic theory of social behavior—a theory in which persons are the active agents, not mysterious forces. Nevertheless, it is also true that the individual acts within limitations set by a physical and social environment, and that these limitations are fit subject for investigation. The division of labor among social scientists set by Asch needs to be recalled here (see Chapter Two, p. 22).

Given the great variation among human beings, it is likely that any given condition, either recognized or unrecognized, will not elicit a monolithic, uniform response from these human beings. Nevertheless, one type of response, or consequence, may be so widespread that we may speak of a high probability that it will occur. This is so even though we are not quite certain of the conditions under which it will not occur, and, therefore, cannot predict the pattern of deviation from the prediction. We thus restrict our attention to aggregate prediction.

Now let us illustrate these notions with the problem at hand. What difference does it make whether two persons live next door

110

to each other or on different planets? The former will probably make some sort of contact with each other while the latter pair, at the current level of technology, will not even know of each other's existence. The contact between the former pair may be rare, anonymous, or hostile, yet we may still state that the probability of contact between these pairs is quite different. Spatial separation, then, places a limitation upon the probability of contact.

By choosing less fanciful sets of persons, we can develop a number of useful propositions about social relationships. In general, as the spatial separation between the homes of two persons declines, the probability of contact between these two persons increases. If we can state the consequences of contact for social relationships, then we have a link between environment and social structure.

Contact of some sort seems to be a prerequisite for a whole host of social-psychological processes. The symbolic processes of communication imply contact. It is quite true that advances in technology permit considerable communication without face-to-face contact. But two other considerations also affect the significance of these technological innovations for our problem.

First, communication without face-to-face contact lacks many of the subtle processes or cues accompanying face-to-face contact. For example, it is quite difficult to gesture meaningfully in a telephone conversation. But these kinds of subtle communication impart much social information. Second, many long-distance communications take place between persons who have previously established face-to-face contacts. The joint effect of these two points is that face-to-face contacts are essential to certain types of communication, that these types of communication impart special kinds of social information, and that many contacts between persons presume prior knowledge of this information.

Therefore, we may argue that particular kinds of social relationships are in fact not increased by technological advances in communication: namely, those kinds of social relationships dependent upon face-to-face communication. Further, we may also argue that these are the typical kinds of social relationships found in our society, and that they are the most significant social relationships in the social structure of a society.

Contrary arguments have been advanced. Some authors believe the average housewife to have more meaningful social relationships with the heroes of soap opera than with members of her own family. Such relationships are widely regarded as symptomatic of current social maladies. In any case, such relationships cannot be regarded as reciprocal or mutual in the usual sense. For our purposes fantasy can be disregarded, though it is not our intention to deny fantasy a leading role in social science.

We argue, then, that the existence of social relationships among types of persons depends upon the existence of contact among members of these types, and that this contact must be, for the most part, face-to-face. Long-distance communication and, for that matter, rapid transportation have been significant in maintaining previously established social relationships as well as in initiating these relationships. But we have defined a stratification system in terms of reciprocal relationships. Therefore, the very existence of a stratification system is dependent upon the existence of contact among the members of society.

In the previous chapter we saw that the usual theories of stratification account quite well for the aggregate spatial distribution of social characteristics. Now, in contrast, we say that the spatial distribution has consequences for the existence of the stratification system, for the kinds of social relationships that exist are in part determined by spatial distribution. Is it possible that this reciprocal relation between social stratification and spatial distribution has a special significance? If we regard a system of stratification as a self-maintaining system, then may we not regard residential distribution as a mechanism or device by which the continuity of the stratification system is ensured in the next generation? Of course, the stratification system is only the result of many actions by many persons, yet the result of these actions may not be fully understood by the persons themselves. Here we may have a regularity that is intended and recognized by some members of society but not necessarily by all.

The relationship between spatial distribution and social relationships may be illustrated by several kinds of data. Studies of informal group formation in newly constructed housing projects provide us with our best information, since a direct observation and measurement of the relevant social-psychological processes is possible. Studies of the relationship between residential proximity and mate selection reveal the behavioral consequences of contact, though the data on the marriage license do not permit further inferences into the nature of this relationship. Finally, observation of social behavior in particular areas of the city enables us to consider the effect of proximity upon the stability of subcultures.

A remarkable study by Festinger, Schachter, and Back brings out the social-psychological consequence of residential proximity (Festinger, *et al.*, 1950). These investigators seized the opportunity presented by the construction of a new housing project for married veteran students at the Massachusetts Institute of Technology in the spring of 1946. The social-psychological processes involved in the development of a new community were thus available for study.

Two characteristics of this community affect any interpretation of the research results. First, social structure did not determine the initial pattern of residential location. The group of married veteran students of engineering was exceedingly homogeneous with respect to the usual sociological variables. Further, the assignment of units was on a "first come, first served" basis, so that the slight variations in social characteristics could not greatly influence the selection of particular housing locations. Second, the community itself was not stable. Residents all regarded it as a temporary place to live, and, in fact, they had been living there less than a year and a half when the main field work was completed.

Since there was no effect of social structure upon location, this research reflects solely the influence of location upon social structure. On one hand, this is highly desirable, for it permits us to determine the effects of location when it operates independently; on the other hand, the homogeneity of the community does not permit generalization to heterogeneous communities, or to homogeneous communities having entirely different social characteristics. We gain clarity but lose generality.

A wide variety of research methods were employed by these investigators. They used "informants, participant and nonparticipant observation, informal and standardized interviewing, sociometry, and field experimentation (Festinger, *et al.*, 1950, p. 10). Thus, the qualitative procedures characteristic of anthropological field work were juxtaposed with the standardized quantitative procedures developed in sociology and psychology. In the analysis, these kinds of data could be related to each other and thus permit conclusions to be drawn that could not follow from the use of one method in isolation.

First, we shall review the relationship between residential proximity and informal group formation in this study. Subsequently, the social-psychological consequences of this informal group structure may be examined.

The effects of proximity were somewhat different in two different parts of the housing development. Separate single-family dwellings were completed first. These were arranged in courts and known as Westgate. Subsequently, two-story barracks containing ten apartments each were completed and arranged in pairs in an adjacent area called Westgate West. The groups that formed in the separate dwelling area reflected the court pattern to a great extent, while floors within apartment buildings tended to become social units in the barracks area.

The data on group formation were collected by a standard sociometric type of interview in which each housewife was asked, "What three people in Westgate or Westgate West do you see most of socially?" (Festinger, *et al.*, 1950, p. 37.) The listing of friends gathered in this way was then related to distance between dwelling units. However, two kinds of considerations entered into the computation of distance. First, direct physical distance between doors of dwelling units was measured. Second, a concept of functional distance was developed to express the positional aspects of architecture and location affecting the paths that people used in walking about the area. Stairway placement in the barracks is an example of an important functional factor affecting functional distance. Both kinds of distance affect the occurrence of the "brief and passive contacts made going to and from home or walking about the neighborhood" (1950, p. 34).

The relationships between sociometric choices and distance are all reported in similar tables and all reveal roughly the same inverse relationship between friendship and distance. Each table for physical distance contains the units of approximately equal physical distance, the total number of choices given between units in each distance category, the total number of possible choices among units within each distance category, and the ratio of choices given to possible choices. The ratio of choices given to possible choices declines as physical distance increases for each of the following tabulations: (1) Distance on one floor of a Westgate West building; (2) Distance between floors of a Westgate West building; (3) Distance between houses in a row in Westgate courts; (4) Location with respect to court for Westgaters; (5) Location with respect to building for Westgate West people.

Tabulations for functional distance contain the positional features of the dwelling unit and the number of choices received by houses in these positions. The end houses of courts receive

115

fewer choices than the intermediate houses, and those end houses facing the street rather than the court receive the lowest number of choices. The position of stairs in the barracks are shown to affect choices within floors as well as choices between floors.

In other words, no matter how the data are presented the effect of physical distance upon friendship patterns is marked. Evidently "passive contacts are a major determinant of friendship and group formation" in these communities (1950, p. 58).

The authors present evidence that the groups defined by these sociometric interviews are social-psychological realities. Attitudes toward a tenant organization in Westgate seemed to be related to court membership and participation in group activities in a court. Those persons who deviated from their own courts in evaluation of the tenant organization also seemed to be relatively isolated by the sociometric criterion. An experiment in rumor planting showed evidence that channels of communication are related to the sociometric structure, especially to cohesiveness of a court defined in terms of a sociometric pattern.

Thus, it seems that in a socially homogeneous student population ecological patterning can determine the growth of friendship relations, which in turn have consequences for group formation. The groups thus formed can exert normative control over their membership in the sense that group standards are formed, which are adhered to by members of the sociometrically defined group.

An independently designed study of student housing at the University of Minnesota corroborates the M.I.T. findings. Caplow and Forman, in 1948, selected a block of fifty dwelling units in a recently constructed student housing project for intensive sociometric study (Caplow and Forman, 1950). The degree of homogeneity and the impermanence of the community are quite similar to that of the M.I.T. student community.

Behavioral, or contact, sociometry was employed in this study. People were asked to state whether they had contact with other persons and to describe the degree of contact according to a prestructured scale. The Westgate findings on physical distance and functional distance were supported in the resulting network of interpersonal relationships. Furthermore, as length of stay in the community increased, the number of acquaintances increased, but the number of close friends did not increase after the first few weeks of residence. This finding supports the view that passive contacts are determined by ecological factors, and that the initial passive contacts grow into the closest relationships through repetition.

These observations of the homogeneous married student housing development are further confirmed by the reports of William H. Whyte, Jr., on the newly developed suburb (Whyte, 1957). While Whyte's research procedures are rather more impressionistic than those discussed above, they do not seem to be distortions of the data. Certain new suburban housing developments, of which Park Forest is an extreme example, tend to attract young married couples with children. The economic, occupational, and social characteristics of these people are much the same. Whyte argues that where there are in fact great differences in social class origin of these people great care is taken to minimize these differences. A group standard of egalitarianism is maintained. Assignment of new housing does not tend to select particular social characteristics in Park Forest save for one part of this subdivision with a markedly different cost.

Thus, the homogeneous, classless characteristics of student housing appear to be reproduced in some of these residential developments. Furthermore, transiency seems to be characteristic of these families. Under these circumstances, the ecological factors noted above are quite effective in determining group formation. Proximity, location in the middle of the block, orientation of dwelling unit, and street plan all seem to affect a wide variety of social activities. The residents suggest that children's play groups have much effect on the formation of parental social groupings.

Further, Whyte argues that these groups patterns lead to dis-

117

tinctive group standards, or subcultures, and that the inhabitants
are fully aware of the processes by which the group standards
arise. Presumably the original inhabitants of these areas were
responsible for the selection of particular group standards. But
Whyte argues that once formed the standards are transmitted to
newcomers, so that an area continues to have the same social
characteristics regardless of the departure of the innovating
pioneer.

Whyte, of course, is bent on demonstrating that the conformity
of the organization man extends even into his home life. Thus,
we may take his comments on suburban conformity with a grain
of salt. Nevertheless, he has engaged in some systematic mapping
of social activities, and sticks sufficiently closely to his unstructured interviewing data, so that one may regard the picture he
draws as accurate.

We may summarize the research on the homogeneous community as proving that, under certain circumstances, ecological
considerations can exercise a determining influence upon the
growth and development of social relations, and of group structure. These special cases, by minimizing the influence of other
social influences, such as social class and ethnicity, permit the
ecological aspects to be clearly seen.

But now, what are the consequences of such results for the
heterogeneous, relatively stable community in which most of us
still live? Addresses on marriage licenses have been mapped by
many investigators. Such data do not allow us to determine the
extent to which they are a consequence of the social-distance
factors, which seem to underlie the ecology of social characteristics or are the direct consequence of spatial location itself.
Nevertheless, by following up samples to obtain further social
information we can see whether either or both of these factors
may be operating.

An article by Katz and Hill reviews, summarizes, and integrates the findings of fourteen of these studies (Katz and Hill, 1958). The original study by Bossard concludes that the proportion of marriages decreases as the distance between the two parties increases. This over-all finding is supported in general by the subsequent studies, though the choice of unit of distance can affect the results somewhat.

If ecological factors of the sort we have been discussing are involved, the probability of contact or a first meeting must be the theoretical mechanism of explanation of these findings. Thus, Bossard and others must assume that the address given on the marriage license is an index of the address at the first meeting of the couple. Obviously, the persons may have changed address during courtship; a particularly difficult situation occurs when both parties list the same address. Clarke checked the change of address pattern by direct interview. His results suggest that moves closer together were about as frequent as moves farther apart. Thus Katz and Hill conclude that the shift of addresses tends to balance out in the aggregated data, although the same-address couples constitute a source of error that is not thereby eliminated.

Some investigators have followed an alternative theoretical route and have attempted to explain these spatial distributions as a result of social distance, as an expression of the social structure, rather than as an ecological phenomenon. Davie and Reeves used New Haven data to test such a theory. They found that 73.6 per cent of marriages were contracted by persons from areas with similar social characteristics. But even so, within groups having the same characteristics proximity seemed to affect mate selection. Subsequently, Kennedy (neé Reeves) tested this latter point and found that ecological factors seem to operate within groups defined culturally as eligible for mates.

The social-distance explanation relies upon two factors: first, that the culture demands marriage with socially proximate individuals; and second, that residential segregation follows the

119

same social-distance pattern as the marriage rules. If a person marries within his own group, and his group is segregated around him, there will be a marked propinquity effect reflected in his choice of mate. If, however, a person deviates from marriage within his own group, he must go beyond the residential boundaries of his own group. Kennedy found that for all ethnic groups in New Haven except the Irish marriages outside of ethnic group were more distant than were marriages within the ethnic group. The exception of the Irish could be due either to the lack of a social-distance marriage rule or to lack of segregation of the Irish.

We do not know which of these factors accounts for the exception of the Irish in New Haven. Nevertheless, the possibility that lack of segregation of a particular characteristic would also result in propinquity effects is suggestive for explaining some other findings in this literature. The less the segregation the greater the distance for culturally approved choices and the less the distance for deviant choices, according to the Katz and Hill interpretation of the combined social distance and ecological postulates. To put it another way, if a social characteristic is distributed randomly, then any value of it may occur close to any particular area. If a person feels free to choose his mate, independent of this social characteristic, then he has plenty of opportunities close at hand. But if he feels restricted to a particular value of this characteristic then he may have to range fairly far afield to satisfy himself. On the average, then, those who must select according to a particular value will display a greater premarital residential distance between mates than those who ignore the characteristic.

The finding of Kennedy and Reeves that the distances between deviant age choices are lower than the distances between conforming age choices can be explained by the absence of age segregation, according to Katz and Hill. Similarly, the finding of several mate-selection studies that low-prestige occupations have shorter premarital residential distances between mates than higher-prestige occupations suggests that segregation is greater for the low-prestige occupations. A similar finding for income levels is also given this interpretation. The finding that education is not related to distance suggests lack of segregation for education. These interpretations are roughly in accord with the findings of the previous chapter, although further research by the methods of Kish mentioned in the previous chapter would establish them more securely.

Katz and Hill conclude by relating the mate-selection behavior patterns to general notions in human migration. They cite Stouffer's hypothesis that "the number of persons going a given distance is directly proportional to the number of opportunities at that distance and inversely proportional to the number of intervening opportunities." If we regard eligible mates as opportunities, then this hypothesis suggests that the number of persons in each eligible category must be considered before the average distance one needs to travel can be predicted. Empirical evidence is cited by Katz and Hill to support this interpretation.

Thus, three principles appear to be jointly at work in these data. First, eligible mates are culturally defined; second, among eligibles, the probability of marriage is related to the probability of interaction; and third, the probability of interaction is limited by the spatial distribution of opportunities or eligibles. In the heterogeneous community, then, social relationships are simultaneously determined by social-distance preferences and ecological factors.

We have now examined the unstable homogeneous community and the over-all city in order to determine the effects of ecology upon social structure. As a final type of community we turn to the relatively stable homogeneous subcommunity. In the previous chapter we saw that cultural preference and discrimination

121

seemed to be major factors in the formation of such subcommunities, and that those formed in response to discrimination seemed more homogeneous than other types of subcommunities. Thus the racial and ethnic subcommunities, and perhaps the lower-class subcommunities in general, seem to be characteristic examples of the stable homogeneous subcommunity.

Is the stability of these homogeneous subcommunities reinforced by proximity? Probably so, but demonstration of this effect and assessment of its significance is not an easy matter. Two types of considerations can be investigated. First, we may examine the notion that proximity affects communication channels and therefore can support interpersonal and intergenerational communication of common cultural beliefs and values. Second, we may examine the idea that particular areas serve a symbolic function, that sentiments attached to these areas are of great significance in the social cohesion of the subcommunity. This symbolic function could not be served, presumably, unless the subcommunity was, in fact, a spatial as well as social entity.

The relationship among proximity, group structure, and communication channels has been dealt with earlier, in the discussion of the M.I.T. housing project. The probability of contact is reflected in the network of interpersonal relationships, which then serves as a determinant of communication channels. If the behavior of the subcommunity is in any sense deviant from the larger society, these communication channels can serve to transmit the deviant culture, for these communication channels should run throughout the spatial unit occupied by the subcommunity.

For example, the ethnic communities of New York and Chicago maintained their own language—for speaking, for newspapers, and even for movies—for many years. Such deviance would have been most difficult if the members of these ethnic groups had been scattered throughout the city in the midst of English-speaking people. Ultimately, the pressures of assimila-

122

tion broke down the language separatism, but the spatial separation surely helped to preserve this language separation for an unusual length of time. With family members, neighbors, storekeepers, church members all speaking the same language and all located together, the older generations could remain sealed off from the larger society without suffering great handicaps in their daily living. Today, the Puerto Rican areas of these cities are again exemplifying this process.

We know that intergenerational cohesion in these areas was not great; that the second and then the third generation turned away from the culture of the parents to the culture of the larger society. But within each generation a cohesion was permitted that was sufficient to preserve much of the deviant culture. Furthermore, the culture that grew up among members of the second or third generation tended to be a youth culture, neither transmitted nor supported by the adult generation. Thus Whyte reports that the corner boys in an Italian slum used the term "greaser" to refer to someone their own age who spoke English with difficulty (Whyte, 1955, p. XX). Yet these same corner boys did not readily assimilate to the settlement house culture provided by the larger society.

The phenomenon of a youth culture is given much attention in *Delinquent Boys* by Albert K. Cohen (Cohen, 1955). The existence of a distinct delinquent subculture is asserted by Cohen. This subculture is transmitted by "differential association," that is, by youths who happen to have many contacts together. One of the factors determining contact is surely ecological. Whyte's observation of corner boys suggests that group formation in a slum area has an ecological basis (Whyte, 1955, p. 3). The young men persist in groups largely reflecting patterns of childhood contact.

But Whyte's data also show that the corner boys become attached to their corner gang, and that they may return to it for some years after their families have moved away; even when the family has moved out to the suburbs (Whyte, 1955, p. 11). It seems likely that it is to the social relationships the boys return rather than to the physical corner. Yet the existence of the corner as symbol must also be recognized. It is not only a convenient meeting place but a way for the gang member to place himself within a society made up of numerous corner gangs.

Thus, we return again to Maine's emphasis upon local contiguity as a basis for group loyalty or cohesion (Maine, 1885). These subcommunities are too large for any individual to know all other individuals. Even if there is a continuous chain of contacts among all persons in the subcommunity, there is no way in which the persons themselves can objectify this larger group. But an area or place name can serve this symbolic function. Often the name itself will suggest its symbolic relationship to the neighborhood or subcommunity. However, as the movement of these subcommunities across the physical face of the city continues the place name need have no reference to the characteristics of the present inhabitants.

The extreme cases of subcommunity identifying with symbolic locale is represented by Beacon Hill in Boston. Here Firey records the tenacity of the beleagured Brahmins, surrounded on all sides by the encroaching Irish (Firey, 1946). The area is not merely symbolic of a group existing in the present. It is symbolic of a whole host of previous generations and of their history. It represents the continuously elevated position of an elite group within the city. Its very historicity is opposed to the fleeting and transient characteristics of much of the rest of urban life. Despite great pressures, the old homes are neither bulldozed into rubble nor subdivided into lucrative slum dwellings. Age is not the sign of infirmity, in this instance, but the necessary requirement for symbolizing past deeds in present times.

Certainly these empirical data do not constitute proof that

proximity reinforces the stability of subcommunities. In this form they are suggestive only.

Yet the cumulative effect of the three kinds of data we have considered is to demonstrate conclusively that the spatial distribution of social characteristics has consequences for social structure. An environmental variable, space, has an effect on social structure. Thus, the evidence for one ecological proposition is established.

The growth and development of social relationships in the unstable homogeneous community is very markedly affected by patterns of location. The role of passive contacts as conditions for the formation of such social relationships is fairly well established.

In the heterogeneous community, with marked distinctions of social distance among various groups, the independent effects of location are not so easily revealed. But a detailed review of the mate-selection literature shows that both social-distance and location effects must be assumed in order to explain the various findings.

More systematic research of a historical and comparative nature is ncessary before the long-term effects of location upon cultural processes can be clearly assessed. Scattered implications of these effects are already available in the literature and are suggestive of the results that further research might obtain.

If the main lines of this analysis are correct, we may think of a stratification system as a self-maintaining system. We know that the location of social characteristics can be predicted in terms of a stratification theory, especially in terms of social distance, and we also know that location itself is a determinant of the subsequent social relationships that will make up the future stratification system.

Undoubtedly, location of residence is not the only consequence of stratification that tends to have the circular effect of reinforcing stratification itself. But the fact that the underlying social distance is not the sole aspect of the stratification system to be transmitted to future generations is worth noting. The situational factors reinforcing social distance are also transmitted. The fact that such processes are for the most part unrecognized in no way detracts from their importance.

7

A Theoretical Model for
Urban Social Structure

WE have defined "social structure" as a persistent system of social relationships, and "stratification" as a persistent ranking system. In the previous two chapters we have examined the mechanisms by which spatial distribution contributes to the maintenance of the system of stratification within a city. We shall broaden our study of the self-maintaining mechanisms in the stratification system, especially those of a social-psychological nature. By broadening our scope we will be better able to comprehend the behavioral consequences of stratification.

127

In order to clarify the nature of the self-maintaining mechanisms, an axiomatic theory, or mathermatical model is being developed. This model will be introduced in essay form in this chapter. Mathematical symbolism will be employed in the Appendix.

The model has three distinctive features: (1) a *single* dimension of stratification is assumed and the logical consequences of this assumption are then investigated—only in this way can we determine the empirical inadequacies of the single-dimension theory and then modify the theory accordingly; (2) the mechanisms for persistence of the stratification system depend upon the marriage patterns of a society—if anyone can marry (or is equally likely to marry) anyone else then there can be no transmission of rank by family to future generations (no monopoly of status symbols by restriction of marriage choice) unless male and female children in the same family are assigned unrelated ranks; (3) this model leads to predictions of individual behavior insofar as individuals maximize their self respect in terms of the stratification system, but at the aggregate level the model also states the limitations on the behavior of those persons who are unaware of or even antagonistic to the system (the system will not be made to disappear by magic).

Let us assume that at an initial time, there exists a hierarchy of classes of families. This assumption defines the stratification system as a hierarchy based on family status. So long as actual families can be ranked or symbols such as occupation can be unequivocally translated into families, this assumption will have a "good fit" with an actual society. Only the hierarchy need be agreed upon, for, as we shall see shortly, under many conditions there must be a lack of consensus with respect to boundaries and to the importance of the hierarchy.

Next we must assume the existence of marriage rules that assign status to the newly formed families at subsequent times, the succeeding generations in our hypothetical population. These marriage rules are necessary for the persistence of the system as defined above. Without marriage rules there could be no system of stratification based on family status.

For applications to the United States we shall assume legal monogamy, and patrilinear status assignment, thus, male status is fixed with respect to the hierarchy. According to these rules, only females may move up or down it. A man may move up only through his grandson, after he has married his daughter up. In actual practice in the United States, status may seem to be more equal between the sexes than the model suggests. However, we can investigate the conditions under which a shift to equality might occur at later times under our model, and we can see that such a shift would alter the stratification system much less than might appear at first glance.

Now let us assume a relatively "closed," persistent system. Although the marriage rules determine status in the next generation unambiguously, they permit a considerable mixing of status in newly formed couples. This mixture can be prevented altogether by requiring couples to marry within classes, but such a completely "closed" system need not be assumed; it is neither realistic nor necessary. Instead, we shall require only that for each class the probability of marriage within class exceeds the probability of marriage in either of the adjacent classes and that this probability declines as the classes become more remote. This requirement will be called the "social-distance condition."

We shall also assume that all parents wish to have their daughters marry a mate higher in status. Later we may consider the conditions under which the parents settle for marrying within their own class. For the moment we must see that the parents simultaneously minimize the probability of marrying down and maximize the probability of marrying up. Thus, the parents in each class emphasize their differences from the class immediately below them and play down their differences from the class immediately above them. To a lesser degree, they emphasize their differences from all lower classes and play down their differences from all higher classes no matter how far removed they are from them.

How do the parents proceed to select their daughter's mate? Arranged marriage would certainly represent the simplest solution, with a dowry used as bait. Let us assume, instead, that the parents seek to control the social structure in such a way that their daughters will have small possibility of meeting an undesirable male. We assume the existence of a hierarchy of social relationships ranging from close to distant. The order of these relationships is determined by the probability that a male having such a relationship with daughter will ultimately marry her. For the American situation, the items on the social-distance scale suggest the appropriate relationships—marriage, eat meals together, same neighborhood, same school, same job, meet on street, and never meet. The parents must either insure that their daughters and an undesirable never meet, or they must invent status inequality. "Status inequality" is defined as an arrangment of the content of each social relationship so that the existence of this relationship between daughter and undesirable does not increase the probability of marriage between daughter and undesirable. Thus, the behavioral content of these unequal social relationships must be culturally defined and socially enforced.

In order to control the content and existence of social relationships, the parents must manipulate institutions and symbols. They must have the power to determine the participation of particular individuals in particular social relationships, which includes the power to determine participation in particular organizations. But in order to enforce these rules of participation they must be able to symbolically differentiate the members of each class. If their power is sufficiently great, they may be able to force the members of each class to wear arbitrary symbols, such as the yellow armbands the Jews were forced to

130

wear under Hitler. But as power declines, the class members must rely on other devices. With little power, the parents' optimum procedure is to choose their symbols in such a way that the boundaries are visible when one looks down upon them from above but invisible to a viewer from below—one-way visibility as with the one-way mirror.

Optimum power monopoly exists with respect to social relationships when the upper classes control the military, legal, political, economic, religious and educational activities, to illustrate with the customary list of Western institutions. (Such a situation was approximated in early medieval Europe.) But the manner in which control is achieved is determined by the general kinds of political restraints or political ground rules admissible in a particular cultural or historical context. Thus, these rules must be supplied before the "game" that the parents play can be defined. As the rules move from authoritarian to democratic the nature of coalitions in this game must be expected to alter. Under an authoritarian system, that is, one in which the social elite maintain optimum political control, we may expect only one type of coalition, namely an agreement on the part of every class to stay in its place. The highest class guarantees the existence of all boundaries in the system in return for a guarantee that its exalted position will not be challenged. We may think of any other class as extorting similar guarantees from less powerful classes. Thus every class will proudly display the symbols of its status, and all classes will subscribe to a common religion that endorses the principle that the happy man is the one who stays in his place. Again, the medieval approximation should be noted.

Symbols of status consist of three categories—material objects, learned behavior, and biological characteristics, especially hereditary biological characteristics. Optimum symbol control exists when the upper classes can maximize the differentiation in society with respect to all three kinds of symbols. In a cash economy the first is determined largely by wealth, the second is determined by the system of socialization, and the biological characteristics are given by the initial selection of members of the society—usually by immigration, though not always by voluntary immigration.

In the United States, the biological symbols differentiate the population into rather marked groups. Since the dominant elite stands at one extreme with respect to skin color it can arrange persons in order according to the degree with which they depart from this standard and then act accordingly toward them. Since these symbols are visible and fixed, they cannot be arranged so as to achieve one-way visibility, and therefore power must be used to maintain status inequality (keep people in their place).

Access to material symbols has become so general in the United States that symbol faking has become a major pastime of the population, especially with respect to automobiles, and clothes. Income distribution is the key to this change. Various tax reforms have helped spread these material symbols around to the general population. Historical data suggests the following speculation. Though these tax reforms have been met by adroit methods of tax avoidance, they have had the result that the elites have felt obliged to engage in more subdued symbol displays so as not to stir up the "masses." Thus, the great displays of wealth of the 1890's vanished after 1910. Democratic political structure has had the result of encouraging inconspicuous consumption, a particularly noticeable transition on the part of the economic elite about whom Veblen wrote. Either material objects that cannot be estimated in price by the general public must be purchased, or the great displays of wealth must be private; the significance of Bermuda as a resort can be appreciated in these terms. It seems unlikely that any elite group can place much confidence today in this form of symbolic differentiation of the population.

The learned symbols have been the bastion of the class system in western Europe. Shaw's *Pygmalion* underlined this point, as did Hardy's *Jude the Obscure*. Nineteenth-century American snobbery was copied directly from the European example, as indeed, has been the case with most American snobbery in any epoch. Certain unique features of the American economy such as the highly developed mass market have made it profitable for certain elite persons to "leak" the learned symbol system to the less favored social levels—as in books on etiquette. The leaking of the systems of aesthetic appreciation has reached such proportions that great shouts of horror at "mass culture" can be heard in the land.

We may deduce the spatial distributions encountered in Chapter 5 as well as the self-maintaining mechanisms of Chapter 6 from the preceding discussion. First of all, we note that undesired contact must either be prevented or controlled. The general method of control is to maintain unequal status in contact situations. The residential patterns of Charleston did not directly reflect "social" distance because unequal status is defined by the Southern cultural patterns. But in the Northern city, unequal status does not receive strong cultural support. Thus, the parents must minimize the probability of contact by whatever indirect means are at their disposal; one of these means today is residential location.

The specific arrangement of different types of groups can be deduced from the following symbolic considerations. If the symbolic difference between two groups is such that one group may become identical with another group if it is aware of the relevant symbols and has access to them, we shall say that the symbolic difference is a *status difference*. If the symbolic difference is further emphasized by an intentional adherence of the lower group to its distinctive objects and customs we shall call it an *ethnic difference*. If the symbolic difference is based upon biological symbols we shall call it a *racial difference*. Clearly, in the United States the probability of symbol faking, or passing,

133

declines as we move from status difference to ethnic difference to racial difference. If, for any particular groups, any two or all three of these conditions hold, the probability of passing will be smaller than that of the component conditions. Thus, the order of ease of passing is: status only, ethnic only, status and ethnic, race only, status and race, ethnic and race, and all three. This proposition can be tested directly by psychological methods measuring the ambiguity of symbols or the "identification" of groups.

If we regard the elite as consisting of white Protestant Anglo-Saxon Americans with high status, then we can predict that the strength of discrimination will increase as the ease of passing decreases. Thus, the groups with status difference alone will be least segregated. Among Negroes and among whites we find that residential status differences exist that can be explained largely by income differences alone. But between Negroes and whites residential differences exist that require additional explanation. But the symbolic differences provide us with an explanation in terms of which all of these residential patterns are merely special cases.

The hypothesis of symbolic differences works rather well for most of the ethnic groups included on the social-distance scale, but the position of the Jews is particularly anomalous. Should they be thought of as a combined case of ethnic and race differences? I think not. Rather, one may suppose at an initial time a class of persons was so regarded by all other classes that intermarriage was clearly prohibited and that the amount of contact with this class was held to a bare minimum. The "pariah" class would be forced to maintain all social relationships with other members of the in-group. Participation in all contacts implying a high probability of marriage must be with members of the in-group. If this system of stratification persists over several generations, a set of customs and beliefs would develop to sanction the group structure in such a way as to preserve the self

134

respect of members of the "pariah" group—thus illustrating Nietzsche's notion of *ressentiment* (Nietzsche, 1918; Briefs, 1937). If the discrimination were relaxed at some much later time, the in-group defense mechanisms would be threatened, since they would seem to be no longer relevant. But those members of the in-group who have vested interests in the persistence of the in-group social structure will resist these changes in the over-all social structure of society. Thus, an extreme degree of ethnicity is created, which departs from the usual "ethnic only" category. The appropriate test for this hypothesis lies in the statistics on intermarriage.

Indeed, the entire system of axioms may be tested by determining whether the degree of residential segregation between any two groups in Northern cities may be predicted from a knowledge of the degree of intermarriage between these two groups. More simply, we must be able to show that social distance as measured by residential statistics can be predicted from social distance as measured by statistics of intermarriage.

We may recall the Katz and Hill paper, (Katz and Hill, 1958). They were able to show that the marital-proximity findings could be reconciled if the degree of segregation could be determined by considering the position of each of these groups in the hierarchy of symbolic differentiation. Neither of these tests have been made to the author's knowledge.

We have now seen that our previous findings can be deduced from an axiomatic theory of social structure. Let us turn our attention to further deductions from this system. Many authors have felt that the lack of consensus with respect to the stratification system was evidence of the absence of stratification. But under the above axioms, if a stratification system persists, lack of consensus must prevail.

Lack of consensus can be deduced from two different considerations. First, if each class chooses to emphasize the next boundary below it and deny the existence of the next boundary above it, differential statements about boundaries will be obtained by interviews of the population. The top group will have a markedly different view from the bottom group. Second, if the top group is manipulating symbols so as to obtain one-way visibility, the bottom group will not be able to describe the boundaries since they will be unaware of them. Thus, there will be no consensus with respect to a stratification system unless the top group holds maximum power (obviating the need for one-way symbols), and this power is employed to maintain an interlocked hierarchy of coalitions of classes aimed at restricting marriage choices to members of one's own class. In other words, if the elite class holds maximum power, the lower classes will take the minimax solution of marrying daughters to equals in return for a guarantee that they cannot marry down. Again, the distinctive class symbols in medieval Europe serve to illustrate the point.

When an elite uses one-way visibility of symbols to help maintain its position, rather restrictive criteria are involved in the selection of appropriate symbols. The symbols must be either invisible or inconspicuous to the eye of the untrained observer. Inconspicuous symbols can be interpreted only by those who have received appropriate training, but this training must be monopolized by the higher classes or the lower class will be able to fake the symbols (Abbot, 1952). Consistent with the terminology of Chapter Three, we may say that the symbols convey information but that the values provide interpretation; thus a monopoly of both symbols and values must be maintained by a higher class in order to use a particular symbol to differentiate themselves from lower classes. Furthermore, when a system contains several classes there must be a cumulative hierarchy of such monopolies in order for the classes to remain symbolically distinct. The highest class must have access to the symbols and values of the lower classes if it is to retain its position securely.

Illustrations of these invisible symbols, as well as illustrations of the differential perspectives of classes, can be given in terms of Warner's six-class system, sometimes known as the "Pullman car" theory of social class (Warner and Lunt, 1941). For literary simplicity we shall refer to class one, class two, and so forth, where Warner refers to upper-upper, lower-upper, upper-middle, lower-middle, upper-lower, and lower-lower, respectively.

Class sixes, at the bottom of the heap, state that the whole system does not exist, or that there are only two or three vaguely defined classes, or that the whole system is based on money alone, which is itself distributed by luck. These people are only aware of the highly visible material objects, such as automobiles, which seem to them to be closely associated with status. If any of these people obtain large sums of money, they are likely to invest it in a very large car. Such people were unable to comprehend the counter-symbol of the small car that the class one's began to use against them.

Class fives have regular jobs and a conception of moral respectability with Protestant ethic overtones. The regularity of work and those aspects of respectability that seem to be associated with regular habits serve to distinguish these people from the class sixes. Absenteeism and its associated causal factors (such as alcohol) are fairly well under control. They are the "respectable poor." For these people stratification is still a rather vague notion, but income is supplemented by certain customs supporting regular behavior in their view of the system. Blue collars and union membership characterize this group occupationally.

The class fours not only have regular jobs, but they wear white collars at these regular jobs. Accompanying the white collar are a whole host of moralisms representing the Protestant ethic in full detail. Class fours engage in church participation, support of the YMCA, the Boy Scouts, and other similar activities. The children are taught quotations from *Poor Richard's*

Almanac and the parable of the ant and the grasshopper. The implication of these tales is that so long as Johnny is a "good boy" he "is just as good as anybody else." Unfortunately for this class, the recent surge of union power has placed them in a precarious position with respect to income. They have arranged their budgets so as to maximize the status characteristics of their housing by tenure, by neighborhood (Duncan and Duncan, 1955) and by interior furnishings. Thus they place emphasis on the symbols appropriate to commensalism (eating meals together) and of neighborhood, and by doing so place themselves favorably with respect to daughters' chances on the marriage market. But they cannot afford the conspicuous symbols of the class fives and class sixes as well, and often grumble among themselves about the unfairness of these circumstances. Fascist movements find ready adherents in this class.

Class threes have more education, more professionalized occupations with more responsible jobs, and a more sophisticated etiquette or "culture" than the class fours. Education and things derivative from education far outweigh the Calvinistic moralisms in this group. A whole host of subtle symbols and subtle gestures are available to these people, many of which are transmitted through college fraternities and sororities, or the college liberal arts curriculum, and then sustained by various community organizations including the service clubs, women's clubs, and various hobby groups. The extensive use of invisible symbols is, of course, accompanied by an elaborate series of indirect tests of status.

Class twos have "social" pretensions. Membership in country clubs, activity on the social circuit, and on the "society" page, are among the characteristics of the class. Extensive elaboration of learned symbols is likely, especially those needed to sustain one's position as a patron of the arts, or theater first-nighter. Daughter must have her junior year abroad, thus permitting her to acquire appropriately esoteric customs and perhaps an appropriately decadent aristocrat as well, while in the United States daughter is closely guarded by a whole host of employees, matrons (house mothers), escorts, social secretaries, and so forth.

Class ones rely upon genealogy for their symbolic distinctions, invisible hereditary biological distinctions. Membership in a Mayflower Club or among the FFV's is not exactly worn on one's sleeve. Only those people who have studied genealogical tables and have learned the names of the significant family lines can determine this status and then only if they are given the name of the person involved. Of course, symbol faking can exist with respect to genealogy, either by changing names or by altering documents.

As we move progressively higher among the classes we see that new symbols must be introduced in order to maintain boundaries, but each higher symbol must be based upon entirely new criteria or its invisibility will be lost. Finally, a higher class must maintain its position with respect to the entire set of symbols used to differentiate it from a lower class or risk loss of its position. Clearly, the symbol monopoly that distinguishes it from the next lower class must be guarded most carefully, for these are the persons who are most likely to attempt to fake this symbol. Persons two classes, and therefore two sets of symbols, down will tend to direct their strategy toward obtaining the nearest symbol. If class one inverts a symbol of class two and class two inverts a symbol of class three, class one and class three have the same symbols, and we say that the system is symmetrical. If we consider the uppers, middles, and lowers as three classes, sex and liquor are examples of symmetrical symbolic behavior. The diffusion of jazz from the lower classes may be partly explained by this symmetry.

Some more main conclusions can be drawn from this summary of Warner's material. It is quite clear that no index based on a single symbol system can reproduce the class system, for invisibility requires the symbol systems to shift. Occupation has relatively clearcut significance as a symbol from class six to class three, but is little help in sorting out class twos and class ones unless the occupation "gentleman" is determined. Since the bulk of the population lies in classes six to three, fairly high correlations between occupation and class will be obtained. But then to equate class with occupation leads to theoretical contradictions like those in the works of Parsons, Davis and Moore, and Barber (Barber, 1957). The functionalist postulate always assumes that there is an interest of society that differs from the interests of the various competing factions in society. There may, in fact, be a minimum set of interests leading to the persistence of a particular social structure, but the have-nots will not feel constrained to preserve that particular social structure. Functionalism resembles a stopping rule for a poker game, the best solution for any individual is to quit while he is ahead, which means that the "haves" always wish to maintain "equilibrium." The fact is that occupation obscures the definition of the elite classes and therefore the appropriate expression of the interests of these classes. Consequently, the use of power or symbol manipulation to maintain the position of the elite is obscured by the functionalist discussion of occupational prestige.

Now let us turn our attention to some psychological aspects of social structure. How is the differential perception of groups related to position in the stratification hierarchy? On the basis of a contact hypothesis, we would predict that the farther apart two groups lie, the less direct information of the other group is available and therefore the greater the tendency for the image of each group to simplify into "stereotypes." Form and Stone report such a finding for social classes in Lansing, Michigan (Form and Stone, 1957). Using open-ended questions, the highest classes showed the greatest degree of certainty in describing the lowest classes, that is, the most distant classes, and the least degree of certainty in describing the class closest to

140

them. Similarly, the lowest classes showed the least degree of certainty for the classes nearest to them. Since the middle classes are closer to either extreme than the other classes: (1) the middle classes have less certainty in their descriptions of other classes than have any of the other classes and (2) the other classes have less certainty in their descriptions of the middle classes than any of the other classes. These results provide us with a rationale for the often reported ambiguous properties of the middle class.

We may now carry this hypothesis over to the ethnic and racial groups. If a lower-class white is closer to an upper-class white than he is to a lower-class Negro, his stereotype of the Negro should be less ambiguous than his stereotype of the upper classes. In order to test this hypothesis we must assume not only a rank order of classes but a metric or distance between each class. This distance may be derived from the probability of marriage between any two groups. As the probability of marriage between two groups increases then the social distance between these two groups decreases until the two groups merge. As the probability of marriage decreases, the probability of a contact in equal status decreases, and the ambiguity of stereotypes between these two groups should decrease.

When we consider the differential perception and differential class symbols some further results of Form and Stone may be deduced. The different bases for the symbols, especially the invisible symbols, leads to the use of different cues for judging class position. Form and Stone found that 78 per cent of lowers relied upon observation and direct interrogation to validate status inferences while over 60 per cent of middles and uppers used indirect interrogation aimed at eliciting subtle cues.

We might further assume that the closer the potential relationship with a stranger, the more the stranger will be evaluated in terms crucial to his acceptance or rejection as daughter's mate. Or to put it another way, the closer the potential relationship with a stranger, the more carefully will symbol faking be guarded against. The symbols that are relatively easily faked, such as cars, clothes, and so on, will be less important in the evaluation, while questions of background, job, morality and so on will be more important. Form and Stone found that more easily faked "appearance" symbols would be relied upon if a stranger were a potential guest only, but that if stranger were involved with daughter the more fixed, or intrinsic, symbols would be relied upon in reaching an evaluation. Goffman delineates numerous strategies for self-presentation in this symbol-faking game (Goffman, 1959).

Now let us consider interview data on the social distance between whites and Negroes when occupation is taken into account. Westie interviewed whites in Indianapolis as to the degree of social distance with Negro doctors, Negro lawyers, and so on down to Negro ditch diggers, including eight occupational categories (Westie, 1952). The higher the status of the white, the greater the differential made between Negroes of different occupational categories, and the closer the average distance of all Negroes to the whites. If we assume that the highest whites are the class threes, then the differential among Negroes with respect to occupational categories may be regarded simply as reflecting the differential significance of occupation among the whites. If we assume that the probability of an equal status contact with Negroes declines as white status increases, then the decrease in average social distance merely represents the maintenance of the same social distance in terms of probability of marriage. This interpretation is supported by further findings of Westie. While two measures of social distance reveal closer average distances for higher-status whites, a measure of desired residential distance, and a measure of desired physical contact yielded equal distances among all whites, no matter what their status. The fact that all whites dislike physical and residential proximity equally can be regarded as expressing equal concern

142

over the probabilities of daughters' marriage. If we recall that the Negro professional will find his clients most likely among other Negroes and least likely among high-status whites then we see that the high-status whites have little to fear from the "closer" social distance.

How can we relate group structure to the stratification hierarchy? Can the in-group, out-group mechanisms be readily approximated to the haves, have-nots mechanisms? A problem of this sort has already been faced in the discussion of the placement of Jews in the social-distance hierarchy. The possibility that a "pariah" group might develop from continuously enforced social sanctions, that this pariah group must then develop in-group social institutions, that special in-group beliefs will develop supporting these social institutions, and that a vested-interest group would gain considerable power over the life of the in-group has already been presented. This vested-interest group will seek to establish self-maintaining mechanisms to preserve the social structure of the larger society. The orthodox Jew must marry within his group. Of course, elites are merely vested-interest have groups.

Nietzsche argued that morality and religion stem from feelings of *ressentiment* on the part of the have-not groups in society. Heaven was a construct introduced to define a millenium, revenge was taken in the form of "the last shall be first and the first shall be last," and all morality was aimed at bringing about this revenge. However, when the have-nots Calvin and Cromwell conquered the elites they set about obtaining this revenge in the present, rather than passively awaiting the Day of Judgment, as Nietzsche implied.

Recently, Albert K. Cohen has stood Nietzsche on his head (Cohen, 1955). In explaining juvenile delinquency in American cities, Cohen argues that have-not resentment of the lower-class boys against the middle-class society leads to antimoral, destructive acts. Putting Cohen and Nietzsche together we have symbol symmetry, for the Calvinist middles invert the upper symbols, while the lowers invert again. Cohen ignores ethnicity in this argument, although his main source of data, *Street Corner Society*, lays great stress upon both class and ethnicity (Whyte, 1955).

Weber also has challenged Nietzsche's argument (Weber, 1946). He states that a "sense of dignity" in socially elite groups leads to an endorsement of the natural conditions of the world; the elites "kingdom is 'of this world'." But the sense of dignity of the have-not status groups "naturally refers to a future lying beyond the present, whether it is of this life or of another."

We may include Weber's argument in our main theoretical structure by assuming that each individual seeks to preserve his own self-respect, and that his self-respect is in part determined by his identification with a symbolically defined unit of the social structure. To the degree that this symbolically defined unit possesses a group structure we may speak of individuals as belonging to in-groups and out-groups. This axiom is an extension of the initial assumption that, in a hierarchy, parents seek to marry their daughter upward.

This "self-respect" axiom can be found in Durkheim's notion that stable future expectations lead to stable self-images (Durkheim, 1951). Festinger's notion of cognitive dissonance expresses a similar thought in modern psychological dress (Festinger, 1957). Merton has expressed the group aspect of self-respect in his concepts of relative deprivation and of reference group (Merton, 1949). Lewin's analysis of self-hatred among have-not in-groups is perhaps the most brilliant use of these notions in contemporary social science (Lewin, 1948). If we recall Lewin's earlier research on levels of aspiration and on group decision processes we may better be able to appreciate his extraordinary contributions.

Merton has stated that the have-not has five possible avenues with which to preserve his self-respect. When presented with a problem situation—a choice among alternatives or a decision—that tends to threaten his self-respect, the individual may accept cultural means and cultural ends—conformity, he may accept cultural ends but reject cultural means—innovation, or he may accept cultural means but reject cultural ends—ritualism, he may reject both cultural means and cultural ends—retreat, or he may seek to change both cultural means and cultural ends—rebellion. Merton argues that most persons, regardless of class, are conformists, that lower-class deviants become innovationists, that lower-middle-class deviants become ritualists, that the middle-class deviants become retreatists, and that the deviant members of a rising class become rebellious.

Merton's entire argument assumes a homogeneous culture initially presented to all classes. This culture, for Merton, consists of success striving for material objects. But neither of these assumptions has much merit. Cohen, whose position represents a recognition of a mixture of innovation and rebellion, demonstrates that the facts of lower-class delinquency bear no relation to Merton's hypothesis. More damaging is the differential values argument of Hyman, the ethnic and racial complications we are discussing, and the dynamics of value change in American history (Hyman, 1953).

Differential values, differential symbolic distinction of groups, differential group structure, differential information, all of these must be taken into account in deriving behavioral consequences from a theory of social structure. Indeed, Merton's concepts of reference group and relative deprivation are of some assistance in this task.

Let us attach a theory of group structure to the axiom of self-respect. We shall say that the number of classes is determined by the number of symbolic distinctions in a society. It is in the self-interest of the elite classes to multiply the number of classes in the system, and in the self-interest of the lower classes to de-

145

crease the number of classes in the system. It is further in the interest of the elites to see that the number of persons in a class decreases as the rank of the class becomes higher, since this situation provides for a minimum of prestige sharing at the top (an analogy to monopolistic tendencies in economic systems). The importance of class membership in determining the self-respect of an individual increases as the number of members of the class decreases and as the rigidity of the symbols identifying the class increases. Thus, elites, ethnic groups, and racial groups tend to develop an in-group structure affecting the self-respect of members. But the have-not in-group members may find themselves in an ambiguous position with respect to the total social structure. As the exclusion of a have-not group from participation in social relationships increases, the extent to which a person's self-respect is determined by membership in that in-group also increases. Orthodox Judaism in the ghettos illustrates the extreme possibilities of this process. If a have-not group is initially excluded, but subsequently permitted increasing participation in the larger system, the member of the have-not group is caught between two possible strategies of increasing self-respect. He may either tend toward the old ways of the in-group, or he may tend toward the new ways of the larger social structure, but if he attempts to tend toward both at once he will be in conflict with himself. Obviously, assimilation processes illustrate this proposition. Sociologists have used the term "marginal man" to describe the person in this predicament. Lewin's description of self-hatred applies to the person who tends toward the larger society, seeks to erase the symbols of the old ways from his person, comes to attack the symbols of the old ways as the causes of his difficulties, selects symbols from the new ways that are diametrically inverted from the symbols of the old ways, experiences guilt, and comes to hate the old in-group and himself. Since the old ways, according to the *ressentiment* hypothesis, represent an inversion of the symbols of the larger social struc-

146

ture, taking on the new ways will probably represent an inversion of the old ways, and thus the individual may have little room for choice in his degree of assimilation. Willy-nilly, he is caught between conflicting symbol systems.

Street Corner Society is the classic empirical proof of Lewin's theory. The peer group necessarily becomes the basis of in-group social structure as an intermediate cultural formation lying between the old ways of the parents and the new ways of the settlement house. The "greaser," who symbolizes the old ways of the parents persisting into the peer group, is as ridiculed as the settlement boy at the other extreme. The peer-group culture must be intermediate and changing, for as each newer generation grows up it must be closer to the new ways than the previous generation. One might predict that loyalty among siblings would be greater in this situation than in either of the extreme situations (all old ways or all new ways).

Let us now imbed our theories of differential values and differential information in this theory of group structure. We shall assume that the probability of value communication between any two persons increases as the closeness of the social relationships between them increases. Thus, a knowledge of the social structure enables us to predict value communication.

We further assume that, for any given person, the values first communicated become determinants of subsequent communication processes. If we regard any unit of communication as a message in a code, then symbolic decoding may be performed utilizing previous information obtained, but the message will be interpreted in its behavioral consequences by previous values obtained (selective perceptions).

From the two previous paragraphs we see the importance to value theory of the Freudian theory of early childhood socialization. The closest relationships exist in the family, and the initial values received exert an influence upon the communication of subsequent values and information. But we need not assume that

147

the initial values themselves are entirely fixed, unchanging, or rigid. The degree of rigidity is itself a variable of some interest.

So far as social structure is concerned, we shall assume that the interests of each class are communicated to the children by the parents, with the degree of insistence upon these interests determined by the cohesiveness of the in-group structure as the value communication from other close relationships will support the value communication of the parents. Since each class in the social structure is socially distant from each other class in the magnitude of the probability of marriage, it follows that value communication will tend to remain within particular classes in subsequent generations. Complete value diffusion between any two classes will result when the probability of marriage between classes becomes sufficiently large, when the two groups become indistinguishable.

We now recall the three general modes of orientation in terms of which decisions can be made. The traditional mode of orientation, in which the selection of alternatives is referred to a source of traditional authority, tends to be found most often in America in some rural areas and in those stable ethnic areas of cities that are bound together by orthodox religions. Generally speaking, this mode is confined to the lower ranges of American social structure, although it is also evident among uppers. The purposive-rational mode of orientation in which selection is made by a pragmatic, individualistic planning criterion is an offspring of the Protestant ethic found widespread among the American middle classes. The short-run hedonistic mode of orientation, in which selection is determined by immediate, situational, individual considerations, is found in those areas of the city in which a traditional mode has lost its group supports but no planning is in evidence. This mode is largely confined to the Warner lower-lowers, or class sixes in our earlier terminology, and is especially characteristic of the downtown "zone in transition" defined by the Chicago school of sociology.

For our immediate purposes we need to notice that the traditional mode tends to be enforced and sustained by group sanctions, that the purposive-rational mode tends to be enforced by internal psychological sanctions, and that the short-run hedonistic mode is enforced by the political and legal sanctions that can be brought to bear on a particular situation. To put it another way, the traditional mode governs behavior through the establishment of group standards or group expectations, which in turn govern the expectations or aspirations of the individuals. The purposive-rational mode governs behavior through the establishment of internal psychological standards that set the context within which the individual extrapolates future expectations. The short-run hedonistic mode does not govern behavior, it is a case of anarchy (Hobbes' postulate) in that factors external to the individual or his group are largely responsible for his choices.

Let us now place the modes of orientation in the context of variables external to the stratification system; political variables, economic variables, and environmental variables. Persons acting in a traditional mode tend to employ a rigid, inflexible strategy in manipulating these variables—insofar as their group structure does not permit flexibility they must adhere to a single strategy regardless of the change in external variables. Persons acting in a purposive-rational mode will tend to calculate the trend of future events in terms of their best prediction of changes in these variables. Furthermore, their estimation procedure is sequential in the sense that they continually revise their estimates of future change and therefore revise their strategy accordingly. Persons acting in a short-run hedonistic mode tend to estimate future events from present events without allowing for change.

We can also see what consequences follow from the external variables for modes of orientation. If the external variables are sufficiently stable so that group structure is maintained, the traditional mode can be maintained (perhaps as a losing strategy). If the external variables are nonrandom, that is, follow some definite pattern, then the purposive-rational mode can be main-

149

tained. But if the external variables are so unstable that neither of these can be maintained, the short-run hedonistic mode is the only available alternative.

Thus, if the external conditions upon which food, sleep, and warm clothing depend are unstable for a particular class, we would expect that a short-run hedonistic mode would be typical in that class. In the United States, money is such a condition and regular employment is the only stable solution available for most of the population. Thus we predict that the irregularly employed poor, namely, the class sixes mentioned above, will act in accordance with a short-run hedonistic mode (Meier and Bell, 1959). If we equate behavior in a short-run hedonistic mode with undeferred gratification, we predict that these people will seek immediate gratification in conspicuous consumption and sex whenever the means become available. Is this the situation existing in Hollywood?

If persons acting within each mode also act to preserve their self-respect, they will emphasize their own virtues, declare the actions of others to be vices, and claim that their own vices are shared by all others. Thus, the class sixes regard the various upper groups as equally materialistic and promiscuous. This proposition can be verified at little expense. At most penny arcades a spectacular melodrama can be viewed (or peeped at) under the general title of "What the Maid Saw Through the Keyhole." The moral of this rather uncouth tale is that no matter how many airs we put on we're all the same underneath.

Perhaps we can now predict which circumstances will lead a person into a particular problem resolution or strategy. Given the class interests, the modes of orientation, and the external conditions we may try to restate Merton's problems. We may define power as access to, or control over, the political and economic variables (and therefore almost all other external variables to the extent that anyone can control them). Any particular decision, then, is a function of the values and information available to a decision-maker at a given time. The differentials by class of values and information plus the in-group, out-group processes provide us with a prediction of the decision that will be reached. But carrying out this decision will require appropriate access to power.

This dilemma can be resolved in the following way. Let us assume that people act in terms of the directions that the course of events shall take. Their knowledge of these directions depends upon their information, their evaluation of these directions depends upon their values, and their way of connecting values and information depends upon their mode of orientation. We shall assume that people act so as to insure that the course of events moves in their direction insofar as they believe it possible to do so. Therefore they use their power so as to insure that the proper course of events takes place. To the degree that any class has power, it will be better able to obtain its ends. This, however, is only a generalization of the assumption that parents seek to marry their daughters upward.

Let us examine only the strategies available in the problem of the daughter's marriage. Parental control of daughter's actions can range from arranged marriage (sanctions in the traditional mode) to daughter's independent choice based on values transmitted to her within the home (sanctions in the purposive-rational mode) to daughter's independent choice based essentially on chance factors (no sanctions). Within these degrees of control we expect to find that arranged marriage will be contracted in terms of an existing system of symbols—genealogical, material, and behavioral; that independent choice with values may include an estimate of long-term changes in the significance of these symbols, emphasizing education today, while anarchic choice will be based upon immediate gratification factors.

Now let us consider parental control over the external variables—power. Independent power is necessary to insure a proper choice of mate for daughter, even though direct control of daughter may be strong. Here we may recall the ordered distance among social relationships through marriage, common meals, same neighborhood, same school, same job, and same city. Considerable power is required to control the more distant relationships. Neighborhood control is achieved by real-estate organizations, by discriminatory bank-lending policies, by "neighborhood protection" agencies, the Ku Klux Klan, and by impromptu mob action. Control over public-school assignment is achieved by neighborhood control plus clever use of zoning (gerrymandering), but if this control is not sufficient to satisfy the more fastidious parents, the private schools are always available. It is extremely difficult to define and control unequal status within a particular public school, although the use of multiple curricula—college prep, commercial, and industrial—in the high schools may have this effect. But control over jobs leads easily to the definition of unequal status due to the rank structure within the organization—so long as all Negro employees are janitors little danger to daughters is incurred by their employment. At the higher social levels—class ones and twos—efforts to control daughters' participation in "social" events leads to the construction of "society."

To the extent that the parents can achieve this control they can protect their own daughters, but such power is differentially distributed. We might expect the uppers to be best able to protect their daughters, and therefore preserve their class "purity," while persons at the bottom half of the scale would be less "fortunate." We note also that the higher the social class of the daughter, the fewer the eligible males, therefore the greater the probability of spinsterhood and the need for extremely stringent controls to convince daughter that no marriage is better than downward marriage. Given static external conditions the traditional elites may retain control, but given changing external conditions, only the purposive-rational elites will defend their position success-

152

fully. This result is not the same that would have been obtained if we considered the differential distribution of modes of orientation.

All these statements must be qualified in terms of the in-group, out-group mechanisms and the resulting operation of traditional sanctions within underprivileged groups. The Orthodox Jewish and Old Order Amish emphasis upon marriage within the group provides a degree of control over daughters and a degree of control over institutional mechanisms comparing favorably with the control that the upper class can exert. Since the extreme sanction for these minority groups is to exclude an individual from the group, the effectiveness of the marriage control depends upon the degree of discrimination exercised by the larger society—if there were no discrimination, exclusion would lose much of its force. Of course, within groups status symbols will also limit the choice of marriage partners, just as within the Negro ghetto in Chicago we find occupational differences in residential areas.

In theory, all classes could approximate groups and a joint decision to marry within each group could be reached as an agreement. The Hindu caste system and the feudal order are said to approximate this situation (Davis, 1951). As indicated earlier, only an extreme concentration of power in the hands of the highest classes could lead to such an agreement. In practice, nearly every system, no matter how rigid in theory, encourages upward mobility of those with desirable hereditary properties, physical strength, physical beauty, and intelligence are examples of such properties. Of course, symbol inversion on the part of the leisure class can lead to the endorsement of physical weakness as a symbol of status.

To the extent that the strategies of marriage are restricted by the diffusion of power among competing groups in the society we see that a certain amount of mobility can take place. The existence of democratic political rules and a rapidly changing

153

economic system tends to limit the degree of control that any one group can exercise acting alone. The need to form complex coalitions among classes coupled with the fact of diverse interests among types of dominant economic organizations severely limits the possibility that any one interest group can maintain a rigid strategy of discrimination. Indeed, only a few strategies are available. The white Southern United States is currently buying time on the way to its defeat in the issue of race relations. The more time the Southerners buy the greater the probability that external conditions might change in their favor. The course of events in the electoral college and in international affairs, however, is currently moving in a direction unfavorable to their interests, and all but the most extreme leaders are resigned to an eventual admission of defeat. This rigid strategy has the undesirable characteristic that little bargaining with other coalitions can take place, and therefore the Southerners can become a political liability. A more effective strategy is to combine three elements appropriately. Members of a class must rank in order the importance of their interests and then study the directional properties of the external variables to determine the likelihood of success in maintaining their interests. They must then always lobby for some interests, bluff and retreat adroitly with respect to other interests, and seek directly to form desirable coalitions by willingness to bargain with certain other interests. Other things being equal, it is best to bargain away that which you know you will lose anyway. This strategy is known as accepting defeat gracefully, so as to win on some other battlefield some other day. The British custom of elevating the sons of wealthy men to the peerage may serve as an illustration.

An especially successful form of mixed strategy is often described as "divide and rule." A special case of this mixed strategy is the "scapegoat" system. An elite group arranges the social structure so that two types of lower classes result. One group is symbolically distinct, ethnically segregated, and stripped of all power to defend itself. The other group may have any or all of the symbolic distinctions, but is usually possessed of some power. Whenever the latter group becomes troublesome the elite group withdraws its protection of the former group, setting it up as a target toward which the hostility of the troublemakers is redirected. Several forms of this game exist, as may be seen in the American South—upper whites, poor whites, and Negroes; Europe—upper classes, lower classes, and Jews; and the Union of South Africa—whites, Africans, and Indians.

The various political and economic tendencies toward equality in the United States meet their most vigorous resistance in the scapegoat games that exist. Negroes, Jews, Catholics, Mexicans, Japanese, Chinese, Puerto Ricans, Indians and hillbillies are among the minorities that may become convenient targets. Several years ago professors found themselves cast in this role.

One might argue that continuous unstructured contacts would lead to the lessening of social distance between these groups, and therefore to a decrease in the probability of successful scape-goating. Yet when we consider the relationships among members of different groups we see the pertinence of the comments of many writers on the fleeting, transient, anonymous conditions of urban social life. To the extent that the members of these groups reside in different areas of the city they will only come into contact during work hours or during trips to the commercial centers of the city. When we consider relationships among members of the same group we find more enduring, permanent social ties.

The different types of contact suggest different psychological characteristics for these kinds of relationships. The anonymous contacts in street crowds or on subways seem devoid of psychological involvement. The content of these contacts appears to consist of recognition of the presence of others, and sufficient recognition of the most gross symbols attached to these persons to permit a sorting of persons into crude categories or types. In a sense these contacts are egalitarian, the subway is a great

155

leveler of relations between persons. Yet the fact that no overt symbols of status difference accompany these contacts does not imply that they in any way disturb the perceived system of status differentials in the city. On the contrary, these contacts tend to support those psychological mechanisms by which the systems of crude categories of persons are maintained and strengthened.

The contacts taking place during work hours are of more enduring psychological significance. Stability of environment and of persons tends to encourage the growth of informal organization, contacts become related to the growth of psychological sentiments in the manner described by Homans (Homans, 1950). Nevertheless, these contacts take place within an organizational system of stratification. Employers are sorted out into various grades and ranks, ordinarily the psychological implications of contact differ according to the degree of similarity of rank of persons in contact. Thus the contacts between workers and supervisory personnel do not have the same psychological implications as the contacts among workers. To the extent that the ranks within the organization correspond to the perceived ranks of these persons outside the organization, contacts within the organization tend to support the over-all system of urban stratification.

According to various studies, the beliefs supporting social distance and scapegoating behavior are destroyed only by special kinds of contact in which members of both groups behave towards each other as if they were equal, in which a degree of personal psychological involvement exists between members of both groups, and in which the minority group members perform tasks which superior group members value and admire (Williams, 1947). Clearly, urban social structure does not permit many of these.

To the extent that skill is becoming a more essential ingredient in our employment policies, there does exist the possibility that some mixture of minority group members throughout the ranks of absentee-owned corporations may take place and provide for egalitarian contacts. Until more equal access to educational facilities is provided for these minority groups, however, this amount of mixing may be of little long-run consequence. The Northerners' fear of physical contact with Negroes, for example, can well be retained along with respect for the accomplishments of a handful of outstanding Negro persons.

My argument is that once a set of symbols is established in a stratification system it is extremely difficult to dislodge them. The properties of "good" symbols of stratification include visibility (two-way racial symbols or one-way status symbols) and rigidity or scarcity. Economists used to be concerned with competition for scarce means, but sociologists are more inclined to say that there would be no competition unless the means were scarce. Both rigidity and scarcity are assured when symbols are monopolized by one class and transmitted by inheritance only. Genealogy and land often have these properties. So long as symbol monopolies are maintained, any old symbol is a good one. Decadent nobles continue to bring a fair price on the marriage market. But if symbol faking develops on a large scale, only the dynamics of fashion can save the upper classes. Again, this is where the villain "mass culture" steps in to disrupt the clever system of one-way visibility of symbols. These processes eroding away the material and behavioral symbols may have the effect of accentuating the remaining biological symbols, especially, in the United States, skin color.

While some members of contemporary elites are not resourceful, others are indeed most clever. In the face of rapid change in symbols of stratification and in the power structures providing control, the elite that adheres to a fixed strategy (acts in a traditional mode) runs a great risk of moving downward in the system. But among the members of the contemporary elite, those who correctly assess the shape of things to come have ample time to adjust accordingly (act in a purposive-rational mode).

157

If education and intelligence will come to have greater significance, these may be bought and married into. If knowledge can be defined as the score one achieves on a test of knowledge of the uppers' invisible symbols, then the uppers are even further entrenched in defense of their lofty position.

In other words, circulation in both personnel and symbols may take place, but the over-all system of stratification may not vanish. Pareto's pessimistic theory of "circulation of elites" may in fact have greater validity than notions of "closed" or "open" societies. In the long run, the personnel may be entirely reshuffled in society. But if we employ three generations as our unit of perceived social structure, then the degree of shuffling is less striking. This proposition may be tested by studying the comparative genealogies of descendants of siblings to determine the degree of mobility with respect to marriage. The old adage of the elites, "shirtsleeves to shirtsleeves in three generations," deserves closer analysis—especially in terms of the manner in which the elites help make the adage come true. Another elite adage, "blood will tell," deserves the same treatment.

This general scheme has now been sketched out with applications to contemporary United States urban social structure. The reader who wishes to see another aspect of this approach should turn to Leach's book (Leach, 1954). The marriage rules, the political system, the economic system, and the groups differ from ours, yet a similar theory of social structure is elaborated. The work of Levi-Strauss is also relevant (Levi-Strauss, 1953).

In the next chapter these notions will be applied to "social organization." Power in particular is dealt with.

8

Urban Social Organization

A theory of urban social structure has now been sketched out. In this final chapter the more general implications of the theory will be examined, and speculation will be given free rein.

First, let us summarize the main features of this approach to urban social structure. The problem was originally narrowed to the study of the over-all network of social relationships. In turn emphasis was placed upon a single aspect of social relationships—social distance. Social distance itself was approached from the point of view of an over-all symbol structure governing social relationships, the systematic arrangement of these

159

symbols in behavior patterns and in belief structures became the focus of attention.

The materials in Chapters Five and Six were aimed at establishing empirical generalizations about urban social structure as defined above. Especial attention was given to the parallels between residential segregation and marriage patterns as they relate to the over-all symbol structure. The implications of social structure for social-psychological processes were also explored in a preliminary way.

The interpretation of empirical materials was the first task in Chapter Seven. The probabilities governing intermarriage became the focus of theoretical attention, and the conceptual apparatus of game theory was borrowed in order to express these probabilities as mathematical functions of different strategies and of differential power. The special strategies involved in symbol selection were investigated in some detail—in particular, the selection of symbols with the property of one-way visibility received close attention. The selection of counter symbols, or the inversion of symbols by adjacent classes, was also given close attention. Thus, the relationships among marriage, symbols, and power is the core of the theoretical development of Chapter Seven.

Social-psychological implications were studied as the second task in Chapter Seven. A theory of group structure was combined with the theory of symbols to obtain implications for the maintenance of self-respect, the problem of self-hatred can thus be treated in the context of symbol selection and symbol inversion. The theory of group structure was then extended to obtain conditions upon the communication process. It was seen that the probabilities of marriage themselves were the crucial conditions upon the communication process, especially upon the communication of values. Therefore, the communication theory was extended to obtain conditions upon a decision theory. If the distribution of values and information throughout a society could be predicted at any point in time, then, it was argued, the decisions of persons in this society could also be predicted.

Chapter Seven closed with consideration of the self-perpetuating mechanisms of urban social structure. Both the flow of symbols to future generations and the social-psychological processes that accompany this flow suggest that many features of social structure tend to persist to future generations. The limiting conditions upon self-perpetuation of social structure were not made explicit; the analysis was tentative rather than definitive. Great theoretical advances are needed in this area.

Nevertheless, speculation as to the general conditions of self-perpetuation (or persistence, or stability, or entropy) may be indulged in without great harm. Such speculation has traditionally been couched in the language of social organization, or social disorganization. The relevant definitional problems were discussed in Chapter Two. We shall now consider several different classical approaches to these problems.

Social organization may be defined in terms of the intermeshing of goal directed activities. In Chapter Two, such a definition was borrowed from Radcliffe-Brown. Thus, the study of social organization first presupposes that relevant activities and goals may be designated. In the light of the designated goals the activities may be studied to determine whether the goals are achieved, and how the goals are achieved.

Two distinct approaches to stability may be dealt with under this definition: first, a functional approach may be employed; second, a power structure approach may be employed.

An orthodox functional approach would require an examination of the conditions necessary for survival of the city. The necessary conditions would be established as goals, and the relevant activities would be defined as those leading to the fulfillment of these goals. Those goals and activities that did not affect the survival of the city would be ignored. Unfortunately, the conditions for survival could not be empirically determined,

161

nor could the relevant activities be sorted by an empirical criterion—the experiments needed to determine survival conditions could not be performed. Little would be learned about the ongoing city—about the processes optimistically directed toward problems other than survival.

A less narrow functional approach would argue that all activities are interrelated, and that therefore all of the activities taking place within the city must be regarded as part of urban social organization. Typically, this line of thought arrives at over-all value cohesion as an antidote to disorganization and, therefore, as the crux of organization. Unfortunately, again, empirical criteria are notably absent from this analysis. The lack of focus of this approach is also disturbing. Specific activities and specific values are seldom mentioned. Relationships among activities and values are asserted, but never demonstrated. Similarly, relationships among various values are asserted but not demonstrated. As yet, this approach yields ambiguous propositions.

We must avoid assuming that any organization or person fully comprehends the consequences of social activities in cities. All of our evidence underlines our own ignorance of such aggregate causal relationships. We need not assume an over-all rational blueprint for behavior, but rather a number of partial blueprints with notable inconsistencies. The goals of the city as seen by the participants must be partial. The fruitfulness of positing any other goals is open to question.

Let us include in social organization those activities explicitly devoted to "municipal" goals. In most cities, one set of activities has crystallized around such goals, the so-called institutions of local government. We shall only introduce other activities as they have explicit consequences for the activities of local government.

Unfortunately, local government is rarely regarded as more than instrumental in determining its own activities. Outside power wielded by pressure groups, factions, interest groups, classes, and so forth is usually regarded as the source and im· petus for the directions in which local government guides the over-all community. The simplicity of the above definition of social organization is largely destroyed by these considerations. We will only consider the activities of city government as effects, but we will not expect to find the relevant causes located within city government itself.

Just what is the nature of power in this context? Is there a power structure, a pattern of relationships among groups with respect to power that is persistent over time? If so, what is the nature of this pattern, a single dimension of decreasing power as within an army, a pair of competing power groups as in Marx, or a large number of more or less evenly balanced factions as in the theory of pluralistic democracy?

The most tenable answer to these questions is that the power structure itself is a variable, that under certain conditions there will be a tendency toward an "authoritarian" power structure, and that under other conditions there will be a tendency toward a "democratic" or even "anarchistic" power structure. The actual power structure prevailing in a particular community must be regarded as a resultant of such conditions, not as a distinctive and permanent feature of the community.

Rossi has discussed some of the conditions relevant to American local government (Rossi, 1959). Roughly, he is concerned with those conditions under which the agencies of local government become brokers between competing power factions and, therefore, come to exercise some independent influence upon the course of events within the community. These conditions reflect the extent to which an elite maintains a power monopoly, at one extreme, and the extent to which power is distributed among two or more social classes at the other extreme. However, Rossi does not specify the external variables which affect the class structure.

Coleman has made a summary study of community conflict

163

(Coleman, 1957). He uses a pluralistic model of competing factions to analyze his data. Two deficiences of his position deserve attention.

First, he is not able to explore the extent to which these factions are part of a persistent power structure. More particularly, the question arises as to whether any specific conflict becomes merely symbolic of long-standing cleavages in a community, the particular issue being lost in the ensuing vituperation. Indeed, the extent to which "issues" are merely pretexts for combat needs to be explored. Much more local historical context is needed to determine whether such factions are ordinarily smoldering beneath the surface of everyday life and to determine whether these factions are related to the type of social structure that we have previously been discussing.

Second, Coleman does not differentiate types of conflict according to the extent to which the well-known cleavages of social structure might be involved. In particular, he does not consider strikes as illustrations of community conflict. Perhaps the following speculation can illuminate the situation. If the outcome of a conflict may affect the probabilities of intermarriage, then factions competing in the conflict will represent the relevant categories of the social structure. More accurately, as the probability that a conflict affects intermarriage increases, then the probability that factions reflect the social structure increases. Thus, we would expect that matters of symbol acquisition such as income distribution or interracial marriage would reflect cleavages in the social structure to a greater degree than would fluoridation of water. Explicit coalition theory may be very helpful in this analysis.

We also need to know such external data as the business cycles in order to evaluate Coleman's work. If Weber's hypothesis of a fluctuation of the importance of class and status is valid, then the community data should reflect it.

Leach has made such conditions central in his study of Kachin

164

political systems (Leach, 1954). He regards all of the local Kachin political systems as moving in an equilibrium from autocratic to democratic forms, or vice versa. A system at either end of this continuum tends to move back toward the other end. But how did these systems arrive at the ends of the continuum?

The Kachin system contains two distinctive political features. On one hand there exists a system of unequal lineages, a class system with a mythological basis for differentiation. On the other hand, there exists an exogamous set of marriage rules expressing the inequalities among lineages, yet also expressing a set of kinship-based political loyalties. Each higher-status lineage is associated with a lower-status lineage to which it gives brides, but a set of reciprocal obligations is also based upon this marriage tie—specifically the higher-status lineage is expected to provide military support for the lower-status lineage. Leach contends that the symmetrical kinship relationship is in contradiction with the asymmetrical class relationships, and that particular types of lineage situations may bring this contradiction out into the open and lead to conflict. If, due to external factors, the system is an autocratic one in which the class lineages are emphasized in a hierarchy of chiefs, then contradictions will lead to a re-emphasis of the symmetrical kinship relations in the political form of independent villages governed by elders and nonhereditary headmen. Conversely, the democratic villages, under pressure from external factors or internal conflicts, will tend to move back toward a system of inequality of rank. Necessarily neither situation is stable or consistent.

The significant external factors are the economic-ecological system and the larger political context. The autocratic, or chief, system requires a surplus of wealth, so that class inequalities may be properly symbolized. The autocratic system is also supported by most types of political relationships with other groups, as inequalities among the larger groups may be symbolized in terms of inequalities of the chiefs of the various groups. The autocratic system is especially appropriate when the Kachins are subordinate, as it simplifies local administration, in this instance by the British Colonial Office.

We cannot expect to find exact parallels to the Burma hills in the American city, but we can attempt to specify analogous elements in social structure and in the external variables. First, let us assume that urban power structure is in large part a reflection of the kind of class system described in the preceding chapter, initially the higher the class, the greater the power. Second, let us assume that some sort of "democratic" political rules exist, which are expressed in terms of election procedures and universal suffrage. If we further assume that the higher the class, the smaller the number of members of a class, then the higher the class the fewer the votes, and we may expect that the power of the higher classes is declining.

Now, power over large numbers of persons, to a great extent, resides in organizations. But many of the powerful organizations in a community may have little or no interest in influencing the local government. Further, the kinds of sanctions available to these organizations may not be especially effective in inducing persons to support particular local political programs. Nevertheless, for any particular organization, there will exist the possibility of involvement in local issues, as is the case with the dental organizations and the fluoridation issue. Normally, many organizations will not seek to influence the community nor to exercise direct control over the political apparatus, yet they will not be totally irrelevant to the political processes.

Now, let us suppose that, due to various historical factors, most American communities were governed by a business and professional elite class during the nineteenth century. In the larger cities this elite merged with an industrial managerial elite. These people could place each other appropriately in rank order, and could therefore cooperate effectively in keeping their subordin-

166

URBAN SOCIAL ORGANIZATION

ates and the tax rate down. Almost all organizations in the community were controlled by members of these elites.

Two challenges have come to these elites. On one hand, the lower classes were grouped by ethnic and racial symbols into political units, segregation created the boss system. On the other hand, common occupational characteristics brought the lower classes together in economic units, the unions. The boss system was aimed directly at control over local political organization, the unions more often dealt in state and national politics, but both tended to become involved in all political levels. They also tended to work together at all political levels, especially under the impetus of the New Deal.

Insofar as power struggles have been aimed at the political process, the two-party system has come to serve as an intermediary organization in the United States. Since the various interest groups cannot successfully launch a party representing their interest alone, they turn their attention to forcing both parties to accede to their demands. The shift from the Prohibition Party of the 1870's to the Anti-Saloon League of the 1900's illustrates this type of strategy. The parties then become brokers, dealing pragmatically with each interest group according to their estimate of its ability to deliver campaign contributions and votes. In order to straddle a sufficient number of issues to win elections, each party must retain an amorphous, if not an ambiguous, public image.

Although each party has been known to engage in various devious procedures, the fact is also clear that, in this century, the Republican voting strength has derived from the party's loyalty to the various business interests, while the Democratic voting appeal has succeeded when the minority groups and unions have given it strong support. Thus, the degree of challenge to the old power structure is partially indexed by the local Democratic vote, at least outside of the South. After the Democratic strength has become sufficiently strong, the local Republican strategy may shift so as to regain a broader voting base, and the index will be less valid. Nevertheless, the point at which the initial Democratic victories, both in local and statewide elections, takes place appears to index the emergence of a novel power structure.

In the emergent power structure, the pragmatic characteristics of the party become far more significant. Sensitive to shifts in issues and voter appeal, the parties choose their strategies in a far more flexible manner. The old guard Republicans stand aghast at each succeeding party convention. Not only flexibility, but also invisibility must be self-consciously employed with great skill.

In political strategies, invisibility extends far beyond mere hypocrisy or ordinary secrecy. The use of "front" organizations or of diversionary tactics also serves to illustrate this principle. In fact, Rossi suggests that voluntary organizations and nonpartisan local politics are both elements in the political strategies of old business elites. Both amount to rear-guard actions, buying time through fronts and through the confusion or concealment of issues. But such rear-guard strategies ordinarily would be jettisoned after defeat.

If a Republican party reorganizes after defeat, the resulting relationships between parties will be less clearly related to social-class lines. A pluralistic model may be appropriate for the relations between the parties. If so, the notions of faction and of interest must be re-examined in order to determine the novel structural features. Probably the parties will be led by different factions among elites.

We must first consider those conditions under which a particular organization must retain rigid strategies, what actions or aims are not available for bargaining. And we must also consider those conditions under which the strategy or allegiance of a particular individual is fixed. Finally, we must examine the latent effects of the pre-existing class alignments—the kinds of effects discussed in Chapter Five.

Our first two questions turn out to be opposite sides of the same coin. For an organization to persist, its strategies must be such that it retains its membership. But if the individual retains his membership in the organization regardless of the organizational strategies, then the individual is employing a rigid strategy. As the members' allegiance strategies become more flexible, the organizational strategies become more circumscribed.

Without consideration of the characteristics of particular individuals we may say that, as the number of alternative organizational memberships increases, each organization must select its strategies within a narrower range. The classic illustration is simply competition on the labor market. In this case, the number of alternative jobs for the worker is in part a function of the number of workers, but as the number of workers declines relative to a fixed number of jobs, the wage strategies of the employer become more circumscribed.

More generally, the number of alternative memberships is a function of the rigidity of membership symbols—or of the conditions of access to symbols. The conditions of access vary according to the characteristics of the symbols themselves—material objects, learned behavior, and genetic conditions—and also according to the previous class system. The marriage probabilities must be known.

So far as the political parties themselves are concerned, the fact that there are only two of them permits great flexibility in strategy selection, as they must only remain preferable to the other party; voter choice is thus greatly restricted. But so far as membership in organizations capable of exerting pressure on the parties the problem is not so simple. The conditions of access to membership vary considerably among these organizations, while the number of memberships held by any particular individual also fluctuates.

One simplification can be made in the problem of organized pressure groups. Assuming that pressure upon parties is dependent upon potential votes and financial support, we may sort the organizations into those with votes only, those with money only, and those with both. If the organization can supply votes, we will further wish to know if it can supply election workers who represent additional potential votes. Roughly speaking, the nationality groups have votes but no money; the unions have votes, voter organization, and money; and businessmen have money, votes, but no voter organization. Thus, there is a tendency for the potential voter strength of an organization to decline as the elite social-class interests of the members increases, and of course, a converse tendency for the amount of money to increase with approach to the elites.

Organizational strategies may be defined in terms of specific proposals presented to the political parties or agencies. Organizations may either initiate or veto such proposals. Now, while the power structure within an organization can determine internal organizational policies when the members have no alternative organization, they can not necessarily control the behavior of members outside of their organizational participation. The unions can retain membership and strength vis-à-vis collective bargaining but be unable to deliver the vote, as in the case of the Taft-Ferguson election in Ohio in 1950. But how is the line drawn between organizationally relevant behavior and nonrelevant behavior? Evidently total absorption of the individual in an organization is possible, as has been suggested in *The Organization Man*. What are the limits to such a process? How is the "legitimacy" of organizational objectives computed by the members? What is the relation among the interests of the members, the interests of the organization, and the class interests?

First, consider any particular act of an individual. If this act has no consequences for other individuals, then it has no consequence for organizations, and therefore we need not consider its relationship to the organizational structure. If the act of an individual affects many individuals, in particular if it requires

170

their cooperation or support, organizational relevance must be considered. A business man does not dare offend his customers, and therefore he does not dare offend the organizations to which his customers belong. The relationship between local newspapers and their advertisers is an especially pertinent example.

If this individual act is interpreted by organizations to be relevant, then they may approve or disapprove. If, further, there is any collusion among organizations, or elite control over all organizations, expressions of disapproval must be such as to both discourage the act and retain the control. If the elite is visible, or in public view, examples can be made of offenders. But if the elite wants to stay under cover, offenders must be hushed up and whisked away.

Now, aside from the unions, all major organizations are controlled by members of the middle classes. If the business elite is unchallenged, the point at which the greatest collective action of organizations takes place is exactly the point at which the issues are drawn clearly in terms of class interest. Thus, the most effective action of community organization is action along class lines. And therefore a pluralistic model of many organizations with quite varied interests is quite consistent with a stratification model. So long as the middle-class organizations "close ranks" when class interests are threatened, both models can be maintained. Thus, Coleman's approach is valid for a broad range of phenomena (Coleman, 1957).

However, the middle-class strategies are somewhat inflexible, due to the ethics that members of this class must display, compared to the invisibility with which the power elite must operate and the need for long-term control. As Coleman points out, the leaders of the opposition in community conflict often are not bound by the need to maintain control in their strategies. In this sense, the leadership is irresponsible and the strategies are flexible. Further, the lower classes are more likely to throw rocks than the middle classes, partly because they are unaware of the

171

consequences of reckless behavior, and partly because they have less to lose. The functionalists' "survival" value has less appeal in the lower classes than in the middle classes.

As the old elite crumbles and new power structures emerge around the competing political parties, a need for more precise research on social cleavage becomes evident. Is the ultimate situation best represented by a single pluralistic model, essentially egalitarian? If not what are the conditions of fluctuation?

The classical social-disorganization theory, already discussed in the opening chapters, dwells on the implications of social relationships for psychological states. The central proposition is derivative from the social psychology of Cooley and Mead, namely, that attitudes toward self are derivative from attitudes of others and that the absence of close social relationships with others leads to an ambiguous self and a confused state of mind. It was then assumed that people in the downtown areas of cities had no close social relationships and therefore had high incidences of mental disease, suicide, and so forth. Thus the absence of close social relationships was believed to lead to a situation in which no network of social relationships could be maintained.

These views have had to be greatly tempered due to the research in *Street Corner Society*, already discussed, and to the work of Wendell Bell and Scott Greer (Meier and Bell, 1959). Evidently people in the slums have friends, and there even seems to be an intensification of emotional social relationships, especially kinship ties, and above all the ties to mother. One line of thought suggests that the harsh slum environment leads to a greater need for such emotional supports that the family serves to cushion the blows of the outside world through an ethnic of sharing. The big city "boss" is often regarded as an extension of the close social relationships known within the family, a further mediating influence. Thus, this line of thought implies

172

that harsh conditions of existence lead to the growth and perpetuation of close social relationships.

Both of these views, however, run into one further difficulty. Common to both views is the assumption that stable, not to say static, psychological states of mind are necessary for the perpetuation of a particular set of social relationships, and are therefore a necessary condition for the perpetuation of any social structure. Such a simple relationship between social structure and psychological states need not be assumed.

It is not change itself that disrupts psychological processes but unexpected change. Thus, if people expect to grow older and assume new roles accordingly, the fountain of youth is unexpected. If a person has a traditional mode of orientation, rapid change in external variables may lead to personality disorganization. But suppose that the source of traditional authority—the Pope, the king, and so forth—should decree change. (For example, the Tsar freed the serfs.) The appropriate behavior for the traditional person is to accept this change, according to the definition of this mode given in Chapter Two.

But the person acting within a purposive-rational mode of orientation is making estimates of future conditions. If his estimates of change are accurate, he is able to act appropriately with regard to change. If unexpected changes occur, however, his behavior may be inappropriate and personality disorganization could result. Data bearing on this point have recently been emphasized by Litwak (Litwak, 1960). If Litwak's position is sustained by subsequent research, ordered change could support a particular social structure rather than destroying all social structures.

The short-run hedonistic mode of orientation, of course, implies the absence of a future orientation. This mode will lead to regularities of behavior if the external situation is stable but will lead to systematic behavior change with systematic change in external variables and to random behavior patterns with random

173

variation in external variables. The implications of this mode for the persistence of social structure thus depend upon the state of the external variables.

This discussion of future expectations and social structure may conclude with a brief remark on the persistence of a single-rank order, or hierarchy, in a social structure. As the power of the elites declines, how can they act so as to retard, and therefore in the long run prevent, a condition of equality?

The correct strategy for the elites is the Smith-Jefferson "payoff," a modern, democratic form of crumb throwing. According to Adam Smith, the only long-term guarantee of rising wages is continued economic growth. Despite the successes of unions in the past few years, the merits of Smith's position still are very great. Once a man has assumed an occupational position he will accept the financial rewards associated with that position, or expected from that position, so long as his material possessions tend to increase, and are not markedly different from those of his neighbors, coworkers, or close associates. Keeping up with the Joneses is good clean fun so long as the outcome is in doubt. The appearance of rising with respect to material symbols is created, despite the fact that the rank order is unaffected.

Thomas Jefferson's support of public education is the other half of the payoff. If a man's children can rise or fall according to their capacity there exists the possibility that his descendants may reach the top. So long as the criteria of capacity are generally accepted, one would expect that the hierarchical arrangement would be accepted. Thus, everyone would have some chance to rise or fall with respect to the symbols derived by education.

Ethnic and racial distinctions would also be affected by the education part of the payoff. Ultimately, the marriage rules determine their position in society, but so far as material symbol acquisition is concerned education is the key. The minority ethnic and racial groups as a whole can only hope to rise (symbolically) through scientific and technical skills; these in turn require edu-

174

cational advantages. The symbols that differentiate ethnic groups from the rest of the population are affected by the strength of ethnic groups internal structure, especially vested interests. Doubtless, the different groups will each be affected by special factors, many of which cannot now be foreseen. The symbolic differentiation of the racial groups will be affected by the distribution of genetic characteristics in the future. If there is little or no intermarriage between racial groups then genetic mixing will continue to reflect extramarital sexual activities. It is difficult at this time to predict the future patterns of either of these components of genetic mixture.

Let us conclude this essay with some half-serious questions, suggestive of the many unsolved problems in our work. Will automation abolish the lower classes, occupationally speaking, to lead to a new dialectical conflict between suburban men and urban machines? Will the doctrine of efficiency in the technological sphere lead to the formation of a scientific-technical elite? Would such an elite benignly promote egalitarianism? Or would they, in the name of science, simply represent a circulation of elites, a shuffling of the personnel and the slogans in the same old system? Will Lord Acton's prophecy, "Power tends to corrupt and absolute power corrupts absolutely," be confirmed by the technical elite? Would you want your daughter to marry a moron?

APPENDIX

Appendix: Mathematical Aspects

I. Some Mathematical Definitions for Stratification

A. We shall assume that at an initial time, T_1, there exists a set of persons such that:

1. All persons are assigned to sets called families, each person having one and only one family, but no restriction on the number of persons in a family.
2. All families are assigned to sets called classes, each family having one and only one class, but no restrictions on the number of families to a class.

3. All classes are ranked from high to low status; let classes be designated $C_1, C_2, \cdots, C_n$, then $C_1 > C_2 \cdots > C_n$. (The relation $>$ is transitive.)

B. At time T_2 (one generation later) new families are formed which are assigned to classes by the following rules:

1. All persons are either male or female.
2. A relation R_1 (marriage) can exist between any male and any female such that one male can be married to only one female and conversely one female can be married to only one male (monogamy). Thus, we may write $C_1 R_1 C_2$ to represent the marriage of a female C_1 to a male C_2, employing a convention of placing the female on the left of the relationship. In general, we have $C_i R_1 C_j$.
3. All persons who are married belong to the same family, this family is assigned to a class in the status hierarchy by a parameter P, where $PC_j + (1 - P)C_i = C_k$ gives the new class C_k. We shall assume $P = 1$ for subsequent development (patrilineal system). Note that no assumption of a metric is needed for $P = 1, 0$, but that a metric between classes must be defined for any other parameter values.
4. We shall represent the assignment of new families to classes by the following matrix of transition probabilities for females:

$$
\begin{array}{c}
\\
T_1
\end{array}
\begin{array}{c}
T_2 \\
\begin{array}{cccc}
C_1 & C_2 & \cdots & C_n
\end{array} \\
\begin{array}{c}
C_1 \\
C_2 \\
\vdots \\
\\
C_n
\end{array}
\begin{array}{cccc}
P_{11} & P_{12} & \cdots & P_{1n} \\
\cdot & & & \cdot \\
\cdot & \cdot & & \cdot \\
\cdot & \cdot & & \cdot \\
\cdot & & & \\
P_{n1} & \cdots & \cdots & P_{nn}
\end{array}
\end{array}
\qquad \sum_{j=1}^{n} P_{ij} = P_{i.} = 1
$$

in which P_{ij} is the probability that a female in class C_i at time 1 will be assigned to Class C_j at time 2 by marriage. By B. 3 above,

180

the corresponding matrix for males is the identity matrix. The transition matrix for one generation is designated P matrix.

C. We shall assume a condition upon the P_{ij}'s such that we have in any row (or column)

$$P_{ii} \geqq P_{i,i+1} \geqq P_{i,i+2} \geqq \cdots \geqq P_{i,n}$$
$$P_{ii} \geqq P_{i,i-1} \geqq P_{i,i-2} \geqq \cdots P_{i1} \ (P_{jj} \geqq P_{j,j+1} \geqq P_{j,j+2}, \text{ etc.}$$
$$P_{jj} \geqq P_{j,j-1}, \text{ etc.})$$

By B. 3. this condition is equivalent to the statement that $P(C_iR_1C_j)$ monotonically decreases as $(i - j)$ increases, since $P(C_iR_1C_j) = P_{ij}$ in the notation of the transition matrix. Matrices satisfying this condition have major diagonal sums d, such that $1 \leqq d \leqq n$. If $d = 1$, then the matrix is a constant, $1/n$, in all cells. All other matrices have d such that $1 < d < n$. Thus, if $i = j$, we have $P_{ij} \geqq 1/n$, while if $i \neq j$, we have $P_{ij} \leqq 1/n$.

D. Let us extend the set of relationships among persons up to, say, in: R_1, R_2, R_3, R_l, R_m. We then extend our assumptions as follows:

1. For only R_l, $P(C_iR_lC_j)$ decreases as $(i - j)$ increases.

2. For $\begin{cases} i \neq j \\ i = j \end{cases}$, $P(C_iR_1C_j) \leqq P(C_iR_2C_j) \leqq \cdots P(C_iR_mC_j)$ $(i, j$ fixed$)$, since $C_iR_1C_j \subset C_iR_2C_j \subset C_iR_3C_j \cdots$

E. To develop a metric for social distance, we consider $P(C_iR_1C_{i+1})$ and $P(C_{i+1}R_1C_i)$, a pair of adjacent classes. If P matrix is symmetrical, then $P_{i,i+1} = P_{i+1,i}$, and therefore the R_1 distance can be unambiguously defined as $P_{i,i+1}$, where $0 \leqq P_{i,i+1} \leqq 1/n$. If $P_{i,i+1} = 1/n$, then there is no distance between C_j and C_{i+1}. If $P_{i,i+1} = 0$, then there is maximum distance between C_i and C_{i+1}. If P matrix is not symmetrical, then upward distance and downward distance must be defined separately. We can compare the distance between pairs of adjacent classes in the form of rank order—thus for upward distance we have $d(C_1, C_2) > d(C_2, C_3)$.

II. Stochastic Processes

Assume that the P matrix is constant for n generations. We can study P^n. What kinds of class systems can be seen at P^∞ and at P^4?

A. Assume that each class can marry into its adjacent classes. Then $P_{i,i+1}$ and $P_{i-1,i}$ are both nonzero, and therefore both diagonals adjacent to the major diagonal contain only nonzero terms.

1. At P^∞ the matrix will consist of a vector, indicating that class position is independent of its initial origin. This result is true no matter what entries are found in the other cells in the matrix—a Markoff chain regular process. (Vanity, Vanity, all is Vanity!)

2. Consider two cases.

(a) All other entries zero: at P^4 the change of class position of C_i descendants will not exceed four steps.

(b) Most other entries nonzero, zeros random by row and column, at P^4 all entries positive: rate of approach to regular can be studied.

B. Assume that one class cannot marry with an adjacent class. If $P_{ij} = j0$ $(j > i)$, then we have an ergodic process. The end state can be partitioned into four submatrices, where the X submatrices are regular:

$$\begin{bmatrix} X & | & 0 \\ \hline 0 & | & X \end{bmatrix}$$

C. Given population inputs and distributions, a more complete study of these processes can be undertaken.

182

III. Tentative Game Model

The entries in the marriage matrix, P, may be represented as functions of certain other variables. We shall describe these functions as an n-person game among the n classes.

At time T_1 there exists a hierarchy of classes, $C_1, C_2, \cdots, C_n$; a hierarchy of symbol vectors associated with each of these classes, $S_1, S_2, \cdots, S_n$; a distribution of sanctions among classes, $S_1', S_2', \cdots, S_n'$; and a desire to marry daughters up (maximize expected symbol acquisition in the next generation) that determines strategy for the parents, acting as a class.

There exists a set of vectors, $S_1^* \cdots S_p^*$, containing all possible symbols and another set of vectors containing all possible sanctions. Each game contains a selection from the symbol space and a selection from the sanction space. The symbols are initially selected in such a way that for every S^* selected there exist elements in all of the class-associated vectors such that these elements monotonically increase (or decrease) from S_1 to S_n. Thus, the selected symbols constitue an $n \times p$ matrix such that the row vectors are associated with classes, while the column vectors are drawn from the symbol space. The sanction S' may be selected from vectors $S^{*'}$ in the same way. Here across any type of $S^{*'}$ the elements are greatest in C_1 and decline in C_n. We have $P(S_i \cdot C_i)_{T1} = 1$ for all $i = 1, \cdots, n$.

Since $P(S_i \cdot C_i)_{T2} = f(S_1', \cdots, S_n')$, sanctions are the mechanisms for allocating symbols in the next generation. There are two kinds of sanctions in $S^{*'}$: rewards, which give expected symbols, and punishments, which take away expected symbols. These sanctions $S^{*'}$ are also divided into two parts, one called the rules (or laws) and the others (less rigid) that are communicated throughout the system and are elements in strategies.

Strategies consist in using sanctions in such a way that expected symbol gain is maximized. Sanctions belonging to any two classes may be summed across, with relative power determined by the resulting ratio. If any two classes both desire the same symbol, or element in a symbol, then $P(S_i \cdot C_i | C_j$ and C_i both want $S_i) = S'_i / S'_j$, assuming both classes throw all their sanctions into the fight. The strategy, then, consists of balancing off sanctions within a coalition structure. We see that C_1 possesses both positive and negative sanctions, but that C_2 possesses only negative sanctions against C_1; in general, if $i < j$, then C_i possesses both positive and negative sanctions, while C_j possesses only negative sanctions. We shall assume that if C_i applies X_1 positive sanctions and X_2 negative sanctions to C_j, the the sum $(X_1 + X_2)$ gives the total number of sanctions applied. However, since positive sanctions amount to giving away symbols, the symbol structure, and therefore the class structure itself, is modified at T_2.

Therefore, a second element of strategy involves the selection of new elements in the symbol vectors from S^*, as well as new elements in the sanction vectors S^*. For example, C_1 may give all of one element in its S_1 vector to C_2, but then obtain a new element for this vector from S^*. It is often easiest to invert the element given away, so that nonmonotonic symbol vectors may be found running across $S_1 \cdots S_n$. Similarly, the negative sanctions applied to C_2 may be so great that $P(S_1 \cdot C_2) = 0$, and then C_2 may invert an element in its symbol vector, refusing to "play the game." New sanctions may also be selected. Different rules may guide these new selections at any time period.

From the point of view of coalitions, the strategy of the "haves" is divide and rule. Thus, instead of pooling their negative sanctions against the "haves," the "have-nots" will use them up against each other. In a linear class system all sanctions may be directed at adjacent classes, thus preventing much change in the system. Thus, the "haves" must preserve linearity and increase the number of classes to achive maximum "divide and rule."

The "haves" must select sanctions such that their monopoly of symbols is maintained. Thus, the "haves" must seek to maximize the symbolic differences between classes, thereby minimizing errors of confusion between classes. Errors of confusion stem from (1) the introduction of ambiguous symbol vectors with respect to the previously selected set of vectors, (2) the faking of symbols, and (3) the stealing of symbols. If all symbols are either property, behavior, or biological hereditary, it may be seen that the biological symbols are hardest to fake or steal and that the new selection rule is governed by genetics from the previous generation, that is, previous reproduction, presumably controlled by previous marriage. From these (and other) considerations the "haves" should move the system towards a complete hereditary, marriage-determined system.

For example, if we argue that the "haves" should select rules such that the system is "monarchical," whereas the "have-nots" should select "democratic" rules, then we see that "monarchical" means political position obtained by genealogy. We may assume that all the rules vectors in $S^{*\prime}$ may be classified into a continuum running from monarchical to democratic, where these rules designate the degree to which C_1 has relative power over any other class. Thus a "rigid," or monolithic, system must have determinate marriages and an extreme sanction monopoly—that is, the two are equivalent (random marriage = anarchy). If democratic rules hold, then "haves" must employ "invisible" symbols (go underground) so that coalitions cannot be formed against them. The rules partially determine the distribution of sanctions, which in turn partially determines the distribution of symbols.

Suppose some sanction vectors in $S^{*\prime}$ are formed in such a way that the number of sanctions is directly proportional to the number of persons in a class. Such sanction vectors define "democratic" voting, for example. Here the coalition problem depends on population processes as well as the symbol and sanction selections. More accurately, the "rules" for voting partially determine the distribution of sanctions.

The selection of symbols at any given play in the game is partially determined by an access function. This function ordinarily differs for property symbols, behavior symbols, and biological symbols. Property symbols are distributed by an economic system, behavior symbols by learning, and biological symbols by genetic processes. These can, of course, all be tied into the marriage rules.

The selection of sanctions also may be studied in terms of different access functions. We may examine the three types—law, custom, and belief—in terms of their distributions throughout the class system. Alternatively, we may regard the distribution of weapons and of organizations as indexing the distribution of sanctions throughout society. For the first alternative we may study the distribution of beliefs through channels of social structure—patterns of contact. If beliefs are composed of values and information, then the communication of these may be determined. If values are communicated through close personal relationships, then the probability of value communication between any two classes increases as the probability of marriage between these two classes increases. For the second alternative, it is conventional to classify organizations as economic, political, religious, educational, and so on. Weapons may be rank-ordered according to their destructiveness.

Now let us consider specific strategies of marriage. Suppose we assume that adjacent classes have opposed strategies for adjacent probabilities of marriage (without regard to the assumptions needed to generate this situation). We need a function to predict the resulting P_{ij}. Let us consider P_{21} in a three-class system.

We shall assume that the C_2 parents act to maximize P_{21}. Therefore, they must control certain events through certain mechanisms. Specifically, they must divide the male population into eligibles and ineligibles and apply differential sanctions to these two sets. If P_{ij} is a function of the number of equal status contacts between an i female and a j male, the parents must

186

maximize the number of eligible-male equal-status contacts with daughter and minimize ineligible-male equal-status contacts.

These acts in turn depend upon the degree of control over the behavior of males, eligible and ineligible (also on control over daughters), and the degree of accuracy with which eligibles can be distinguished from ineligibles.

Degree of control may be expressed in terms of a *relative power function* or *sanction access function* for classes, which in turn is composed of sanctions. Three kinds of sanctions are available: (1) legal sanctions—expressed in the legal structure and applied by "police" agencies—(2) group sanctions—expressed only in custom and applied by those who accept the customs—and (3) psychological sanctions expressed in beliefs and values and applied internally as "guilt." Ordinarily, all three must operate together, but in the South

$$\begin{cases} C_1 \text{ has } (1) + (3) \\ C_2 \text{ has } (2) \end{cases}$$

The accuracy of distinction between eligibles and ineligibles is determined by the *symbol-access function,* which is itself partly determined by the relative power function. Several types of power relations may be considered.

Type 1—arranged marriage. Here the parents completely control selection of mates. A dowry is used to bargain for the sons-in-law, and cash equivalents are established for marrying up, marrying in, and marrying down. Thus, the utilities (eligibilities) function can be numerically estimated. If the distribution of income by family and the distribution of status by family can be jointly determined, the directions of movement of daughter can be predicted.

(a) Let us assume that the overt display of symbols in such a society is based on cash only and that an annual income necessary for the appropriate display can be estimated for each rank.

187

Then a stable equilibrium of cash and status can be established—thus, equilibrium should predict the dowry equivalents. Income distribution thus serves to estimate the symbol-access function. If inheritance laws specify men only, and ownership laws specify men only, then men only bargain for dowries—patriarchal and patrilineal together.

(b) Assume that biological symbols also assign status in this society. Note that the transmission of biological symbols is symmetric with respect to sex, so that the woman who marries up with cash carries with her the inferior symbol and transmits it according to genetic probabilities on to the next generation. Thus, either caste lines form according to biological symbols or mixture is permitted and expressed explicitly in the utilities, perhaps in dowries—see Brazil as an example of a mixture.

Type 2—parents and daughters together. Here the parents have certain controls over daughter's behavior and mate selection, but the error in these controls is large enough to require the cooperation of the daughter in order to assure success. This cooperation is most easily obtained by teaching the daughter to believe those things that you believe—especially what defines a "nice" boy. Errors in the learning process must be estimated.

For this type the key is segregation, not bargaining. The social contacts in the society may be rank-ordered in terms of the probability of marriage resulting between the daughter and a male as a consequence of this contact. Thus, we order relationships $R_1, R_2, \cdots, R_m$, with R_1 being marriage itself. We expect that a series of ritually defined equal-contact situations are part of the customs in any society—eating meals together (commensalism) is usually R_2. After the equal contacts are ranked, or partially ranked, the ritually defined unequal-contact relationships must be ranked (servants). If no contact at all takes place, $P(C_iR_mC_j) = 0$, then all other contact probabilities are zero, and therefore the probability of marriage is zero.

188

Thus, the parents' best strategy is to arrange the social relationships such that the most eligible (or highest utility) males have the highest probabilities of close contact and the least eligible males have the lowest probabilities of any kind of contact. Let us consider the constraints upon this strategy.

The parents are constrained by (1) the relative strength of their sanctions and (2) their ability to accurately differentiate symbolically the eligibles from the ineligibles (an estimating function). For (1) we may consider an arbitrary pair of adjacent classes. For (2) we must express the accuracy of estimation partly as determined by sanctions.

Let us consider several cases:

(a) C_i has great control over the behavior of C_{i+1}, where C_i is clearly distinguished from $C_i + 1$. In this case the C_i strategy is to make C_{i+1} "stay in its place," that is, keep away from daughter. Thus, legal sanctions, group pressure (lynchings), and belief systems (myths, values, and super-ego) will all be directed to this end, with the extreme results that $C_i + 1$ may be defined as nonhuman (Southern slaves). Extreme segregation is enforced by sanctions on both C_i and $C_i + 1$.

(b) C_i has little control over the behavior of C_{i+1} but has great control over the symbol-access function that differentiates C_i from C_{i+1}. Then C_i must segregate itself from C_{i+1}, using internal cohesion (joint actions) and maintaining control over the symbol-access function. Thus, the C_i sanctions must be applied to the C_i persons in order to maintain segregation. The belief that C_{i+1} *prefers* to live by itself (be segregated) will be espoused by C_i.

(c) C_i has little control over C_{i+1} and little control over symbol-access function. Then C_i must invent invisible symbols, but the leaking of such symbols leads to faking. Thus, it is difficult to apply sanctions, since the degree of error in punishment may be great. This case leads to considerable flow of fashion—

diffusion of symbols. The rates of flow become a crucial area of investigation.

Type 3. C_i has no control over C_{i+1}, little control over fellow members of C_i, and little control over symbol-access function. Daughter must be taught the principles of the game, then she is on her own. The problem is to correctly estimate the changes taking place in the status system and therefore choose mates by criteria that will be rewarded in a novel emerging status system (technology and education).

Both type 1 and type 2 can be further differentiated according to the form of the symbol-access function. Given sufficient control by C_i, arbitrary symbols can be assigned (yellow armbands), but under less control, the symbols are themselves produced by another system and assignment of symbols only is available for control. Consider cases:

(a) Symbols are assigned by marriage selection (for instance, biological, inheritance of property). Here, if C_i can hold $P(C_i R_1 C_{i+1})$ to zero, then there will be no mixing of symbols in future generations. By sex symmetry, biological symbols must be controlled through $P(C_{i+1} R_1 C_i)$ as well, and all illegitimate births must be assigned downwards, whereas inheritance by males only makes $P(C_{i + 1} R_1 C_i)$ indifferent to symbol distribution.

(b) Symbols are assigned by a mechanism not wholly or necessarily tied into marriage selection. Insofar as property is acquired through income, then income distribution determines symbol access, and we must determine the extent of control of classes over income distribution. Insofar as appropriate status behavior is acquired through formal education, we must determine the extent of control of classes over the distribution of students by schools or the mechanism for the selection of students. The distribution of occupation and career choices raise similar problems. Note that insofar as career choice is left to the student, the parents' value instillation affects the selection mechanism. In each case

190

the mechanism must be specified and the class control through sanctions identified.

Once control over the symbol-access function is determined, there still remains the quality of the product to discuss. How well the symbols differentiate the population can be studied in terms of how easy it is to fake status, that is, in terms of perception alone. We therefore need to solve two problems: (1) acquisition of symbols discussed above and (2) ambiguities of symbols.

A number of special topics can be analyzed with this approach. The explicit mathematics has not yet been written for these cases, so we may regard them as problems for which the author does not provide the answer.

The cases already discussed in the text are amenable to this treatment. Both the United States urban social structure and the Southern United States social structure may be represented by distributions of symbols and sanctions, and the prospects for these structures may be investigated under the hypothesis of new symbol and sanction inputs. In both cases exogenous sanctions must be considered as part of the rules—international relations specifically.

The hypothetical society in Edwin Abbot's *Flatland* should be generated by this approach. Indeed this approach was inferred from *Flatland* and the two kinds of structure mentioned above. Other utopias should be generated by this approach, and general methods for determining the consistency of utopias should be developed.

Other kinds of hierarchies may be studied. The rank order of universities and the academic marketplace may be studied as a case of symbol payoff, as, indeed, may any prestige market problem. International relations—the rank order of nations—may be studied also. Two questions need examination: Should we let the Russians marry our daughters? Why should anyone blow up our wealth if they can steal it? Crumb throwing of the Smith-Jefferson payoff type is pertinent here.

191

The whole equilibrium problem posed by Leach is amenable to this approach. Under what conditions do societies (or groups) shift from monarchical rules to democratic rules? Can the decay of an absolutist system be programmed on a computer? The following problems could be investigated: (1) the decline of feudalism, (2) the coalition structure of revolutions and the conditions for success, (3) the decline of Stalinism, (4) American politics as a coalition problem. Of special interest is the concept of rigid and flexible social systems in which a rigid system is threatened by change—even random change. The American Constitution defines a flexible society—it may be studied in terms of its optimum properties for a flexible (or open) society.

Perhaps the reader can now construct further problems, as well as seek explicit solutions to the problems presented. The author welcomes correspondence on these subjects.

REFERENCES

References

Abbot, Edwin. *Flatland*. New York: Dover Publications, Inc., 1952.
Alihan, Milla Aissa. *Social Ecology: A Critical Analysis*. New York: Columbia University Press, 1938.
Asch, Solomon. *Social Psychology*. Englewood Cliffs, N.J.: Prentice-Hall, Inc., 1952.
Barber, Bernard. *Social Stratification*. New York: Harcourt, Brace & World, Inc., 1957.
Bates, Frederick L. "Position, Role, and Status: A Reformulation of Concepts," *Social Forces*, 34 (May, 1956).
Bell, Wendell. "Economic, Family, and Ethnic Status," *American Sociological Review*, 20 (February, 1955), 45.
Bendix, Reinhard, and Seymour Martin Lipset. "Karl Marx' Theory of Social Classes," in Reinhard Bendix and Seymour Martin Lipset (eds.), *Class, Status, and Power*. Glencoe: Free Press, 1953.

Berlin, Isaiah. *Karl Marx, His Life and Environment*. London: Butterworth, 1939.
Beshers, James M. "Census Tract Data and Social Structure: A Methodological Analysis." Unpublished Ph.D. thesis, University of North Carolina, 1957.
———. "Statistical Methods for Small Area Data," *Social Forces*, 38 (May, 1960).
Bogardus, Emory S. *Immigration and Race Attitudes*. Boston: D. C. Heath & Company, 1928.
Briefs, Goetz A. *The Proletariat*. New York: McGraw-Hill Book Co., Inc., 1937.
Broom, Leonard and Philip Selznick. *Sociology*. Evanston, Ill.: Row Peterson & Company, 1955.
Browne, Waldo R. *Altgeld of Illinois*. New York: Huebsch, 1924.
Burgess, Ernest W. "The Growth of the City: An Introduction to a Research Project," in Robert E. Park, Ernest W. Burgess, and Roderick D. McKenzie (eds.), *The City*. Chicago: University of Chicago Press, 1925. Pp. 47–62.
Caplow, Theodore, and Robert Forman. "Neighborhood Interaction in a Homogeneous Community," *American Sociological Review*, 15 (June, 1950), 357–367.
Centers, Richard. *The Psychology of Social Classes*. Princeton: Princeton University Press, 1949.
Cheyney, Edward P. *The Dawn of a New Era*. New York: Harper & Brothers, 1936.
Cohen, Albert K. *Delinquent Boys: The Culture of the Gang*. Glencoe: Free Press, 1955.
Cohen, Albert K. "The Study of Social Disorganization and Deviant Behavior," in Robert K. Merton (ed.), *Sociology Today*. New York: Basic Books, Inc., 1959.
Coleman, James S. *Community Conflict*. Glencoe: Free Press, 1957.
Davis, Kingsley. *Human Society*. New York: The Macmillan Co., 1948.
———. *The Population of India and Pakistan*. Princeton: Princeton University Press, 1951.
———, and Hilda Hertz Golden. "Urbanization and the Development of Pre-Industrial Areas," *Economic Development and Cultural Change*, 3 (October, 1954), 6–26. Reprinted in Paul K. Hatt and Albert J. Reiss, Jr. (eds.), *Cities and Society*. Glencoe: Free Press, 1957.

196

———, and Wilbert E. Moore. "Some Principles of Stratification," *American Sociological Review*, 10 (April, 1945), 242–249.

Dollard, John. *Caste and Class in a Southern Town*. New Haven: Yale University Press, 1937.

Duncan, Otis Dudley. "Human Ecology and Population Studies," in Philip M. Hauser and Otis Dudley Duncan (eds.), *The Study of Population*. Chicago: University of Chicago Press, 1959.

———, and Beverly Duncan. *The Negro Population of Chicago*. Chicago: University of Chicago Press, 1957.

———, and Beverly Duncan. "Residential Distribution and Occupational Stratification," *American Journal of Sociology*, 60 (March, 1955), 493. Reprinted in Hatt and Reiss, *op. cit.*, pp. 283–296.

———, and Stanley Lieberson. "Ethnic Segregation and Assimilation," *American Journal of Sociology*, 64 (January, 1959), 364–374.

Durkheim, Emile. *The Division of Labor in Society*. Trans., George Simpson. Glencoe: Free Press, 1947.

———. *The Rules of Sociological Method*. Trans., Sarah A. Solvay, and John H. Mueller, ed., George E. Catlin. Glencoe, Illinois: The Free Press, 1950.

———. *Suicide*. Trans., John A. Spaulding and George Simpson. Glencoe: Free Press, 1951.

Festinger, Leon. *A Theory of Cognitive Dissonance*. Evanston, Ill.: Row Peterson & Company, 1957.

———, Stanley Schachter, and Kurt Back. *Social Pressures in Informal Groups*. New York: Harper, 1950.

Figgis, J. N. *Studies of Political Thought from Gerson to Grotius*. Cambridge: Cambridge University Press, 1956.

Firey, Walter. *Land Use in Central Boston*. Cambridge: Harvard University Press, 1946.

Form, William H. "The Place of Social Structure in the Determination of Land Use: Some Implications for a Theory of Urban Ecology," *Social Forces*, 32 (May, 1954), 317–324.

Form, William H., and Gregory P. Stone. "Urbanism, Anonymity, and Status Symbolism," *American Journal of Sociology* 62 (March, 1957), 504–514.

The Editors of *Fortune*. *The Exploding Metropolis*. Garden City, N.Y.: Doubleday & Company, Inc., 1958.

Goffman, Erving. *The Presentation of Self in Everyday Life.* Garden City, N.Y.: Doubleday & Company, Inc., 1959.

Gordon, Milton. *Social Class in American Sociology.* Durham, N.C.: Duke University Press, 1958.

Greer, Scott A. *Last Man In.* Glencoe: Free Press, 1959.

Hatt, Paul K., and Albert J. Reiss, Jr. (eds.) *Cities and Society,* Glencoe: Free Press, 1957

Hawley, Amos H. *Human Ecology.* New York: The Ronald Press Company, 1950.

Hollingshead, August B. *Elmtown's Youth.* New York: John Wiley & Sons, Inc., 1949

Homans, George C. *The Human Group.* New York: Harcourt, Brace, 1950.

Hoyt, Homer. *The Structure and Growth of Residential Neighborhoods in American Cities.* Washington, D.C.: Federal Housing Administration, 1939.

Hunter, Floyd. *Community Power Structure.* Chapel Hill: University of North Carolina Press, 1953.

Hyman, Herbert. "The Values Systems of Different Classes," in Reinhard Bendix and Seymour Martin Lipset (eds.), *Class, Status, and Power.* Glencoe: Free Press, 1953. Pp. 426–441.

Katz, Alvin M., and Reuben Hill. "Residential Propinquity and Marital Selection: A Review of Theory, Method, and Fact," *Marriage and Family Living,* 20 (February, 1958), 27–35.

Kahl, Joseph A. *The American Class Structure.* New York: Holt, Rinehart & Winston, Inc., 1957.

Kish, Leslie. "Variance Components of Population Characteristics." Paper read at the meetings of the Population Association of America, Brown University, 1959.

Kollmorgen, Walter. "The Agricultural Stability of the Old Order Amish and Old Order Mennonites of Lancaster County, Pennsylvania," *American Journal of Sociology,* 49 (November, 1943), 233–241.

Leach, E. R. *Political Systems of Highland Burma.* Cambridge: Harvard University Press, 1954.

Lenz, John W. "Hume's Defense of Causal Inference," *Journal of the History of Ideas,* 4 (October, 1958), 559.

Levi-Strauss, Claude. "Social Structure," in A. L. Kroeber (ed.), *Anthropology Today.* Chicago: University of Chicago Press, 1953. Pp. 524–553.

Lewin, Kurt. "The Conflict between Aristotelian and Galilean Modes of Thought in Contemporary Psychology," in *A Dynamic Theory of Personality*. Trans. by Donald K. Adams and Karl E. Zemer. New York and London: McGraw-Hill Book Co., Inc., 1935.

———. "Self-hatred among Jews," in *Resolving Social Conflicts*. New York: Harper & Brothers, 1948. Pp. 186–201.

Lipset, Seymour Martin. *Political Man.* Garden City, N.Y.: Doubleday & Company, Inc., 1960.

Litwak, Eugene. "Reference Groups Theory, Bureaucratic Career, and Neighborhood Primary Group Cohesion," *Sociometry*, 23, No. 1 (March, 1960), 72–84.

Lubell, Samuel. *The Future of American Politics*. Garden City, N.Y.: Doubleday & Company, Inc., 1956.

Lynd, Robert S., and Helen Merrell Lynd. *Middletown*. New York: Harcourt, Brace & World, Inc., 1929.

Mack, Raymond W. "Housing As an Index of Social Class," *Social Forces*, 29 (May, 1951), 391–400.

Maine, Sir Henry. *Ancient Law*, 5th ed. New York: Holt, Rinehart & Winston, Inc., 1885.

Meier, Dorothy L., & Wendell Bell. "Anomia and Differential Access to the Achievement of Life Goals," *American Sociological Review*, 24, No. 2 (April, 1959), 189–202.

Merton, Robert K. "Manifest and Latent Functions," in *Social Theory and Social Structure*. Glencoe: Free Press, 1949.

———. *Social Theory and Social Structure*. Cited in Chap. II.

Mills, C. Wright. "The Middle Classes in Middle-Sized Cities," *American Sociological Review*, 11 (October, 1946), 520–529.

Mitford, Nancy (ed.). *Noblesse Oblige*. London: H. Hamilton, 1956.

Myers, Jerome K. "Ecological and Social Systems of a Community," *American Sociological Review*, 15 (June, 1950), 367–373.

Myrdal, Gunnar. *An American Dilemma*. New York: Harper & Brothers, 1944.

Nagel, Ernest. "A Formalization of Functionalism," in Ernest Nagel, *Logic Without Metaphysics*. Glencoe: Free Press, 1956.

Nef, J. U. *Industry and Government in France and England, 1540–1640*. Philadelphia: American Philosophical Society, 1940.

Nietzsche, Friedrich. *The Genealogy of Morals*. Trans., Horace B. Samuel. New York: Boni and Liveright, 1918.

North, Cecil C., and Paul K. Hatt. "Jobs and Occupations: A Popular Evaluation," *Opinion News* (September 1, 1947), pp. 3–13.

Northrup, Herbert R. *Organized Labor and the Negro*. New York: Harper & Brothers, 1944.

Odegard, Peter H. *Pressure Politics: The Story of the Anti-Saloon League*. New York: Columbia University Press, 1928.

Park, Robert E. *Human Communities*. Glencoe: Free Press, 1952.

Parsons, Talcott. *The Social System*. Glencoe: Free Press, 1951.

———. *The Structure of Social Action*. Glencoe: Free Press, 1949.

Pirenne, Henri. *Medieval Cities*. Garden City, N.Y.: Doubleday & Company, Inc., 1956.

Radcliffe-Brown, A. R. *Structure and Function in Primitive Society*. Glenco: Free Press 1952.

Renard, G., and G. Weulersse. *Life and Work in Modern Europe*. New York: Alfred A. Knopf, Inc., 1926.

Riesman, David. *The Lonely Crowd*. New Haven: Yale University Press, 1950.

Rogoff, Natalie. *Recent Trends in Urban Occupational Mobility*. Glencoe: Free Press, 1953.

Roper, Elmo. "Fortune Survey of Public Opinion," *Fortune* (February, 1940).

Rossi, Peter H. *Why Families Move*. Glencoe: Free Press, 1955.

———. "A Theory of Community Structure." Paper read at the 1959 Annual Meeting of the American Sociological Association, September, 1959.

Schmid, Calvin F. *Social Trends in Seattle*. Seattle: University of Washington Press, 1944.

Schnore, Leo F. "Social Morphology and Human Ecology," *American Journal of Sociology*, 63 (May, 1958), 620–634.

Shevky, Eshref, and Wendell Bell. *Social Area Analysis*. Stanford: Stanford University Press, 1955.

Simon, Herbert A. *Models of Man*. New York: Wiley, 1957.

Simpson, Richard L. "A Modification of the Functional Theory of Social Stratification," *Social Forces*, 35 (December, 1956), 132–137.

Sjoberg, Gideon. "Comparative Urban Sociology," in Robert K. Merton, Leonard Broom, and Leonard S. Cottrell, Jr. (eds.), *Sociology Today*. New York: Basic Books, 1959. Chap. XV.

———. "The Preindustrial City." *American Journal of Sociology*, 60 (March, 1955), 438–445.

Smith, Adam. *The Wealth of Nations*. New York: Random House, 1937.

Smith, Henry Nash. *Virgin Land.* New York: Vintage Books, 1957.

Tryon, Robert C. *Identification of Social Areas by Cluster Analysis.* Berkeley and Los Angeles: University of California Press, 1955.

Ulman, Lloyd. *The Rise of the National Trade Union.* Cambridge: Harvard University Press, 1955.

United States Bureau of the Census. *U.S. census of population: 1950, Vol. III, Census Tract Statistics.* Washington, D.C.: U.S. Government Printing Office, 1952.

Van Arsdol, Jr., Maurice D., Santo F. Camilleri, and Calvin F. Schmid. "The Generality of Urban Social Area Indexes," *American Sociological Review,* 23 (June, 1958).

Veblen, Thorstein. *The Theory of the Leisure Class.* New York: The Viking Press, Inc., 1931.

Warner, W. Lloyd, and Paul S. Lunt. *The Social Life of a Modern Community.* New Haven: Yale, 1941.

————, et al. *Democracy in Jonesville.* New York: Harper & Brothers, 1949.

————, Marchia Meeker, and Kenneth Eells. *Social class in America.* Chicago: Science Research Associates, Inc., 1949.

————, and Leo Srole. *The Social Systems of American Ethnic Groups.* ("Yankee City Series," Vol. III.) New Haven: Yale University Press, 1945.

Weber, Max. "Class, Status, and Party," in Hans Gerth and C. Wright Mills (eds.), *Max Weber: essays in sociology.* Oxford: Oxford University Press, 1946.

————. *The City.* Glencoe: Free Press, 1958.

————. *The Protestant Ethic and the Spirit of Capitalism.* London: George Allen and Unwin, 1930.

————. *The Theory of Social and Economic Organization.* Glencoe: Free Press, 1947.

West, James. *Plainville, U.S.A.* New York: Columbia University Press, 1945.

Westie, Frank R. "Negro-White Status Differentials and Social Distance," *American Sociological Review,* 17, No. 5 (October, 1952), 550–558.

Whyte, William Foote. *Street corner society.* Chicago: University of Chicago Press, 1942, 2nd ed., 1955.

Whyte, William H., Jr. *The Organization Man.* New York: Simon and Schuster, Inc., 1957.

201

Williams, Robin. *The Reduction of Intergroup Tensions.* New York: Social Science Research Council, 1947.

Wirth, Louis. *The Ghetto.* Chicago: University of Chicago Press, 1928.

———. "Urbanism As a Way of Life," *American Journal of Sociology*, 44 (July, 1938). Reprinted in Hatt and Reiss, *op. cit.*

Young, Michael, and Peter Willmott. *Family and Kinship in East London.* London: Routledge and Kegan, Paul, 1957.

INDEX

Index

Abbot, Edwin, 136
Aggregate problem, 14, 30–32, 59
Alihan, Milla Aissa, 60
Anomie. 8, 49
Asch, Solomon, 22

Barber. Bernard, 52, 140
Bates, Frederick L., 44
Behavioral system, 22
Bell, Wendell, 90–91, 93, 104, 150, 172
Beshers, James M., 90–91, 94, 96, 101
Bogardus, Emory S., 50, 99
Bossard, James H. S., 119

Briefs, Goetz A., 72, 78, 80, 135
Broom, Leonard, 56
Browne, Waldo R., 83
Burgess, Ernest W., 94, 101

Caplow, Theodore, 116
Causal relationships, 9, 10, 16, 18, 27, 110, 162
Centers, Richard, 42
Cheyney, Edward P., 68
City, 14, 57
Cohen, Albert K., 19, 123, 143
Coleman, James S., 163–164, 171
Community, 14
Cultural system, 21

205

Davie, Maurice R., 119
Davis, Kingsley, 42, 46, 64, 140, 153
Decision, 32–33
Dollard, John, 105
Duncan, Otis Dudley, 26, 96–100, 102, 138
Durkheim, Emile, 5, 14, 26, 31, 39, 48, 144

Economic system, 24
Endogenous variable, 18
Environment-organism relationship, 24
Environmental system, 21
Equilibrium, 18, 20
Event, 16
Exogenous variable, 18

Festinger, Leon, 113–115, 144
Figgis, J. N., 64
Firey, Walter, 25, 95, 124
Form, William H., 25, 95, 140
Forman, Robert, 116
Functionalism, 13, 15, 22, 26, 40, 51, 140, 172

Goffman, Erving, 142
Gordon, Milton, 46
Greer, Scott A., 80

Hatt, Paul K., 42, 50
Hawley, Amos H., 14, 21, 88
Hill, Reuben, 119–121, 135
Hollingshead, August B., 41
Homans, George C., 156
Hoyt, Homer, 94, 96, 99, 106
Hunter, Floyd, 42, 45, 54
Hyman, Herbert, 145

Kahl, Joseph A., 37, 92
Katz, Alvin M., 119–121, 135
Kennedy, Ruby Jo Reeves, 119–120

Kish, Leslie, 104, 121
Kollmorgen, Walter, 59

Latent functions, 28, 109
Leach, E. R., 37, 39, 48, 57, 158, 164–165
Lenz, John W., 16
Levi-Strauss, Claude, 37, 39, 158
Lewin, Kurt, 17, 144, 147
Lieberson, Stanley, 98–99
Lipset, Seymour Martin, 54
Litwak, Eugene, 173
Lubell, Samuel, 77–78, 80, 83
Lynd, Robert S., 54

Mack, Raymond W., 15
Maine, Sir Henry, 62, 64, 84, 105, 124
Malthus, Thomas R., 25, 29–30
Manifest functions, 28, 109
Marginal man, 146
Marx, Karl, 40, 62
Mass culture, 43
Measurement, 17
Mechanical solidarity, 5, 33
Meier, Dorothy L., 150, 172
Merton, Robert K., 15, 18, 26–27, 29–30, 144–145
Mills, C. Wright, 42
Mitford, Lady Nancy, 74
Mode of orientation, 33–34
Moore, Wilbert E., 42, 140
Myers, Jerome K., 98
Myrdal, Gunnar, 70, 82

Nagel, Ernest, 28
Nef, John U., 72
Nietzsche, Friedrich, 135
Norm, 44, 46
North, Cecil C., 42, 50
Northrup, Herbert R., 80

Odegard, Peter H., 5
Organic solidarity, 5

Pareto, Vilfredo, 40, 158
Park, Robert E., 23–24
Parsons, Talcott, 14, 20, 40, 44, 88, 140
Pirenne, Henri, 64–67
Power, 53–54
Process, 17

Radcliffe-Brown, A. R., 20, 39, 42–43, 105, 161
Reeves, Ruby Jo, 119–120
Renard, G., 71, 73
Riesman, David, 79
Rogoff, Natalie, 83
Roper, Elmo, 77
Rossi, Peter H., 101–102, 163, 168
Rule, 44, 46

Schmid, Calvin F., 94
Schnore, Leo F., 26
Self-fulfilling prophecy, 29
Self-maintaining mechanism, 128, 133
Selznick, Philip, 56
Shevky, Eshref, 90–91, 93, 104
Simmel, Georg, 60
Simon, Herbert A., 18, 29
Simpson, Richard L., 42
Sjoberg, Gideon, 3, 64–65
Smith, Adam, 75
Smith, Henry Nash, 4, 76
Social desirability, 102
Social disorganization, 7–8, 20, 49, 172
Social distance, 25, 50–51, 56, 63–64, 74, 84, 91, 100, 102, 118, 120, 125–126, 130, 135, 142, 155, 159
Social organization, 8, 19–21

Social relationship, 21, 23, 35, 39, 46, 49, 57, 112, 130, 172
Social stratification, 35–37, 40–41, 44, 47, 48, 51–57, 112
Social structure, 19–21, 35, 38–39, 41, 43, 45, 47–48, 53, 55, 57, 59, 61–62, 96, 135
Socialization process, 55
Stone, Gregory, 140
Structure, 16, 42
Symbiotic relationship, 23
Symbols of status, 130–131, 136, 157
System, 18

Thomas, W. I., 29
Tönnies, Ferdinand, 7
Tryon, Robert C., 90

Values, 33, 54–57
Van Arsdol, Maurice D., Jr., 90
Veblen, Thorstein, 51, 132

Warner, W. Lloyd, 15, 42, 53, 58, 82, 136, 148
Weber, Max, 40, 43, 51, 64–69, 85, 92, 144, 164
West, James, 77
Westie, Frank R., 142
Weulersse, G., 71, 73
Whyte, William Foote, 56, 81, 98, 123–124, 144, 147, 172
Whyte, William H., Jr., 52, 117, 170
Williams, Robin, 156
Willmott, Peter, 45
Wirth, Louis, 65, 98

Young, Michael, 45